Salt & Pepper Shakers Made in the USA

Sylvia Tompkins
and Irene Thornburg

Schiffer
Publishing Ltd ®

4880 Lower Valley Road, Atglen, PA 19310 USA

Designed by Joseph M. Riggio Jr.
Type set in header font Van Dijk/text font Korinna BT

ISBN: 0-7643-2077-7
Printed in China
1 2 3 4

Published by Schiffer Publishing Ltd.
4880 Lower Valley Road
Atglen, PA 19310
Phone: (610) 593-1777; Fax: (610) 593-2002
E-mail: Info@schifferbooks.com

For the largest selection of fine reference books on this and related subjects, please visit our web site at **www.schifferbooks.com**
We are always looking for people to write books on new and related subjects. If you have an idea for a book please contact us at the above address.

This book may be purchased from the publisher.
Include $3.95 for shipping.
Please try your bookstore first.
You may write for a free catalog.

In Europe, Schiffer books are distributed by
Bushwood Books
6 Marksbury Ave.
Kew Gardens
Surrey TW9 4JF England
Phone: 44 (0) 20 8392-8585; Fax: 44 (0) 20 8392-9876
E-mail: info@bushwoodbooks.co.uk
Free postage in the U.K., Europe; air mail at cost.

Contents

Acknowledgements

We sincerely appreciate the assistance and encouragement of friends and collectors, especially the following contributors to this book: Nailah Azzam-Zeeveld, Diane and Ralph Bass, Nancee Brewer, Carol and Ross Campbell, Trish Claar, Kathy Cowlishaw, Ava Ezell, Bob Gentile, Shirley Gimondo, Lorraine Haywood, Betty and Freddie Hunter, Julie Low, Mona Low, Clara and Hubert McHugh, Jean Moon, Joyce Porter, Joanne Rose, Sabra Sattler, Bonnie Schwitzgable, Marcia Smith, Rose and Charlie Snyder, Lynda Thornburg and Rusty Johannson, Karen Weaver, Ruth and Ken Wittlief, and Betsy Zalewski.

Special thanks goes to George Higby for providing valuable new information on Treasure Craft and to Don and Norma Winton for their contributions on Twin Winton and Hirsch Manufacturing Co.

Introduction

This is the third book by the authors on American-made ceramic salt and pepper shaker sets made in the mid-20th century. Here are hundreds of sets, made in California and elsewhere, by important manufacturers. Sets by Arcadia, California Originals, William H. Hirsch Manufacturing Co., Metlox Potteries, Treasure Craft, Pottery Craft, Twin Winton, F & F Mold and Die Works, McCoy Pottery, Rossware, Trevewood, and Rick Wisecarver are featured. Some of these companies produced sets with a "wood finish," so the opportunity to compare similarities and differences is at hand.

The discovery, by collector and author George A Higby, of a 1952 Treasure Craft catalog was fortuitous. It is excerpted here to provide answers to the long-standing questions about what company made a large number of flat-and-unglazed bottom go-with sets.

Trevewood Pottery also made several similar sets, in fact in some cases the same items, so it is very hard to know who the actual manufacturer was. With the help of many other collectors, this work attempts to identify the proper makers of each set shown.

Arcadia Ceramics, best known for their minis, also produced many other shakers, such as fruits, vegetables, condiments and three-piece sets.

The value ranges shown in this book are an average compiled from contributors, reference material, internet auctions, and the authors' experiences. As always, values are intended only as a guide. The values will vary based on condition, geographical location, knowledge of the seller and buyer, and sometimes pure luck.

The Novelty Salt and Pepper Shakers Club is an international organization of 1,000 collector-members, who enjoy the friendship and benefits derived from joining with others who share a love of their hobby . Twenty-four regional chapters (twenty-two U.S. and two Canadian) afford an opportunity for collectors to get together with other members in their region. Each year the club's convention is held in a different region to give as many members as possible a chance to attend. Quarterly newsletters provide information on shaker identification and history, and offer a means to buy, sell, and trade. For information about the club, please contact the authors.

Part 1

California Potteries

Chapter 1

Arcadia Ceramics

The History of Arcadia Ceramics, Inc.
by Marcia Smith

The salt and pepper shaker collector's love for the tiny go-together "mini" shakers inspired the hunt for information on the Arcadia Ceramic Company . Through the research process, I have talked with and received pictures and letters from many interesting and helpful people. My first contact was a librarian employed by the City of Arcadia Public Library. I learned from her that the Arcadia Ceramic Company first appeared in the city directory in 1950 with Alfred L. and Esther Johnson as owners. The company was located on St. Joseph Street in Arcadia, California. I eventually learned that some years later, Mr. Johnson was killed in an airplane accident and Mrs. Johnson no higher lives in California.

The 1952 city directory showed the company was still located in Arcadia but the owner names had changed to John T. Bennett, president, and John Renaker, secretary/treasurer, and the name had been changed to Arcadia Ceramics, Inc. I was able to locate the then-president, John Bennett. Mr. Bennett has taken the time to answer my many questions and to give me the benefit of his wit and his memory. Unfortunately, most company records have disappeared over the years and we may never know all the sets they produced.

Much to my surprise, I found that the Johnsons produced no miniature shaker sets under the Arcadia Ceramic name, but are credited with the production of the three-piece sets, which were usually designed by Esther Johnson.

After the purchase of the company and its original molds, the new owners continued to produce these popular sets for at least a year. Bennett and Renaker phased out this series with the hope that their detailed, multi-colored "mini" shaker line would bring new interest to their company. They began production of the now-very-collectible "minis," and the vegetable and fruit sets known to the two men as "the big ones." They are also credited with the production of the three-piece stump sets, such as the owls, squirrels, bears and (my favorite) the ladybird and nest of eggs on a stump. The stumps and sets came in a variety of colors and animal types, but the identifying characteristic common to each set is that the S/P holes are the animals' eyes, either round or crescent-shaped.

Arcadia Ceramics, Inc. also manufactured animal sets, such as owls, pelicans, and dodo birds, designed to be a more expensive line, full-sized, and trimmed in gold. These sets are not often seen in collections, but originally bore the Arcadia label, helping us to identify them. All sets produced were marked with a paper label of some type, bearing the company name. The exceptions are the "minis," simply because they were so small that there was no room for a label. However, the optional dome package did have the company name stamped on the bottom.

Arcadia Ceramics, Inc. did not limit their production to just shakers. One of Mr. Bennett's favorite items was his set of four cantaloupe dishes with saucers. The 1958 city directory shows that George Good had been added as vice-president and the company had moved to Monrovia, California. The 1960 directory showed no listing for Arcadia Ceramics, Inc. I learned from Mr. Bennett that the company closed its doors during 1958.

More Arcadia Ceramics Identified
by Carol Campbell

More sets made and distributed by Arcadia Ceramics have been discovered and identified, either by sticker labels or by Mr. Bennett, former president of the company.

Needless to say, the best method of identification is to find sets with the labels affixed. These labels came in three known styles:

round, green with white print
round, yellow with brown print
square, green with gold print and edges

The square label was more commonly found on the three-piece sets and on larger sets, like the Orientals.

According to Mr. Bennett, it was the "customer's choice" as to how shakers were paired with their base, in some three-piece sets.

It was in 1987 that I was first in contact with Mr. Bennett, who has been most helpful in answering my questions about the shakers and the company in general. It was from Mr. Bennett that I learned that the very popular minis were only produced "from early 1951 through 1958." Mr. John Renaker (a silent partner with Mr. Bennett) stated, "Arcadia made some other decorative accessories, including a collection of life-size vegetables to be used as a wall ornament."

Shown below are a variety of trays designed for use with the shakers at the customer's option.

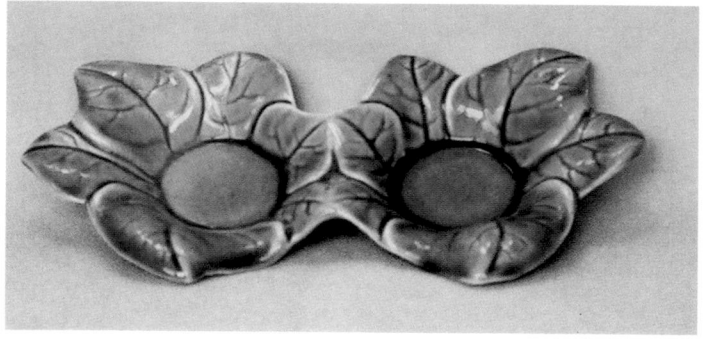

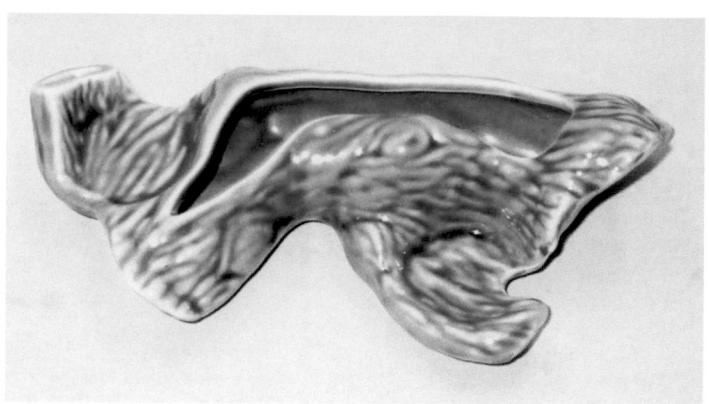

8" long

5" long

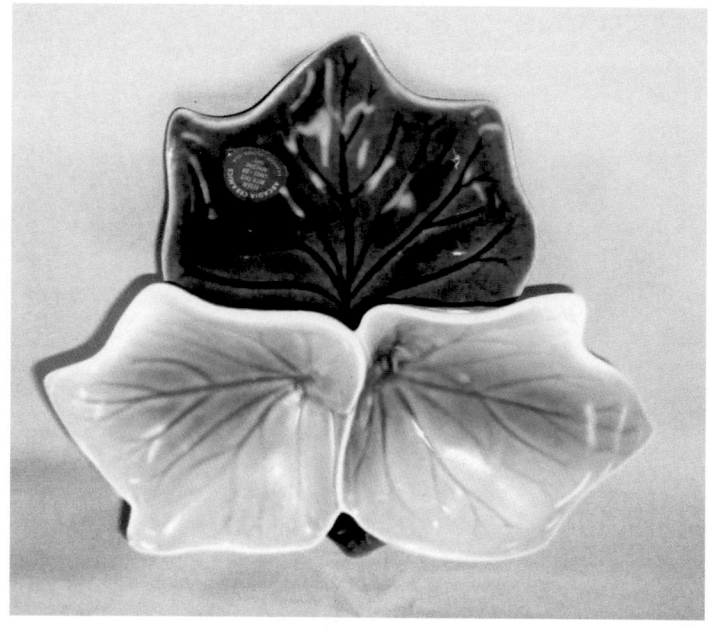

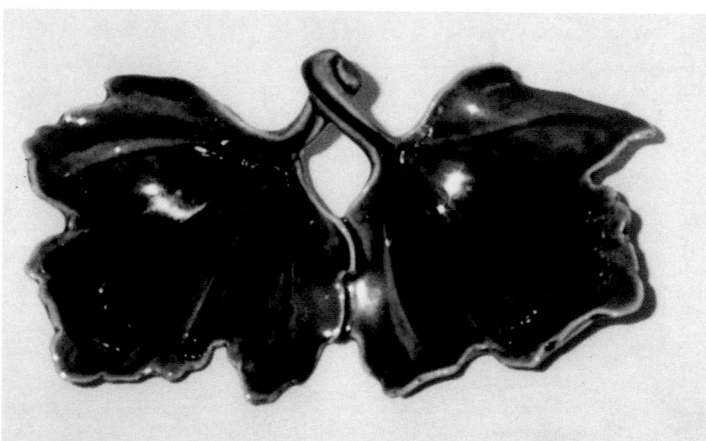

5" long

8" long

8" long

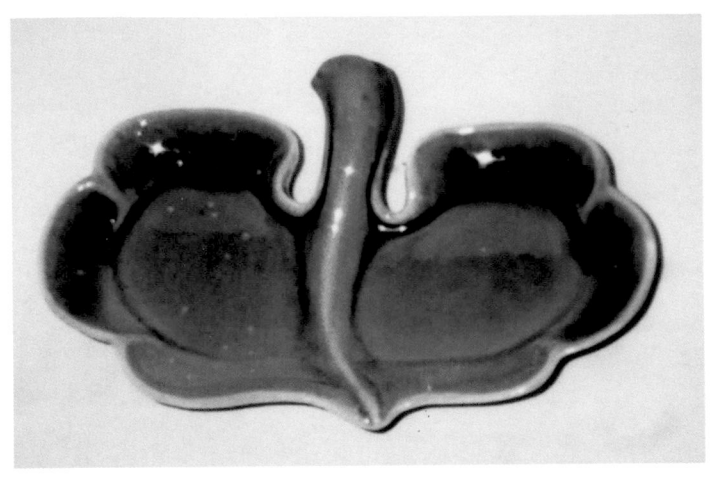

5" long

Courting Crows. 3.75" high. $30-35.

Owl and pelican. 3.5" high. $30-35.

6" long

5" long

Penguins. 3.5" high. $30-35.

Shakers are priced on a stump or tray. Add $5 for the stump with a red bird attached.

Bears. 4" high. $15-18.

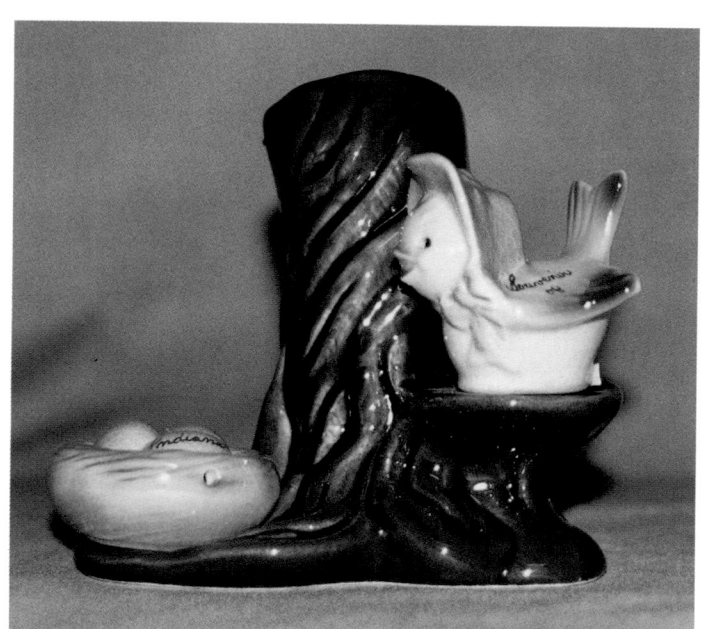 

Lady bird & nest. 4" high. $18-20.

Squirrels. 3" high - 4" high. $18-20.

Foxes. 4" high. $18-20.

Owls. 4" high. $18-20.

Elves. 3" high - 4" high. $18-20.

Hen with eggs. 3" high. $18-20.

Rooster with eggs. 3.5" high. $18-20. To be correctly paired, the eggs should be smaller than the rooster, according to Mr. Bennett.

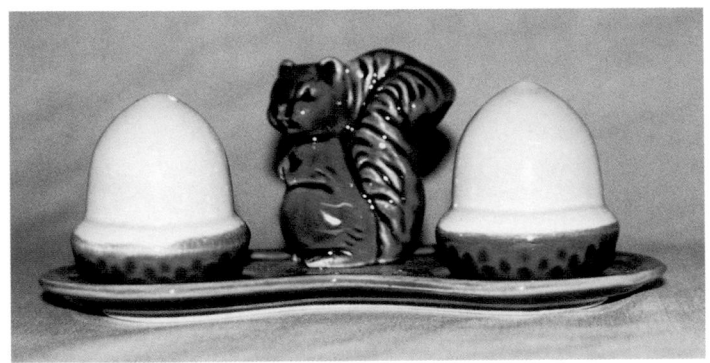

Squirrel with acorns or walnuts. 3" high. $18-20.

Swan with cygnets. 3.5" high. $30-35.

Swan with flowers. 3.5" high. $30-35.

Elves. 3.25" high. $18-20.

Dutch boy or girl. 3.5" high. $25-30.

Hawaiian girl. 3.75" high. $25-30.

Mexican boy. 3.75" high. $25-30.

Dutch couple. 4.75" high. $30-35.

Girl with flowers. 4.5" high. $30-35. Note: the set found with girl in pink is a copy, not made by Arcadia, according to Mr. Bennett.

Orientals.
5" high. $30-35.

Orientals with gold trim. 5" high. $35-40.

Orientals with toothpick holder. 2.5" high. $30-35.

Hispanics. 5" high. $35-40.

Fireplace with logs. 3.75" high. $30-35.

Clown condiment. 3.5" high. $30-35. Priced as complete set.

Soldiers condiment. 3.5" high. $30-35.

Orientals condiment. 3.5" high $30-35.

Fruits and Vegetables

Fruits and vegetables are priced, as usually found, without a tray. Add $5 for a small tray, $10 for large, and $15 for two-tone.

Apple and pear. 2.5" high. $10-12.

Cantaloupe. 1.5" high. $10-12.

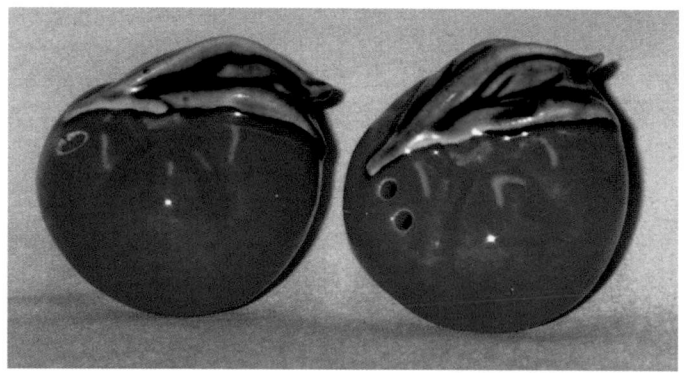

Oranges. 2" high. $12-15.

Figs. 2" high. $10-12.

Apples. 2" high. $12-15.

Watermelons. 1.5" high. $10-12.

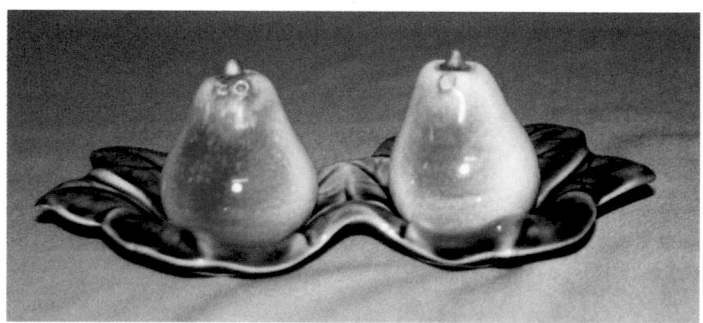

Pears. 2.5" high. $10-12.

Pineapples. 4" high. $12-15.

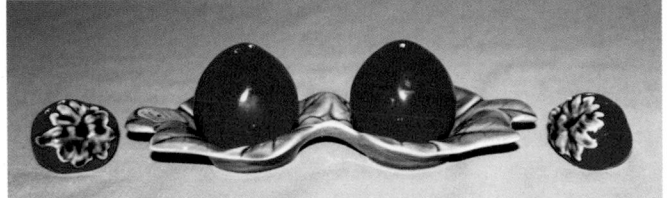

Strawberries. 1.5" high. $12-15.

Artichoke. 2" high. $12-15.

Strawberries, shown with small jar. 1" high. Not priced.

Wheelbarrow with pumpkins, squash or cabbage. 2.5" high $20-25.

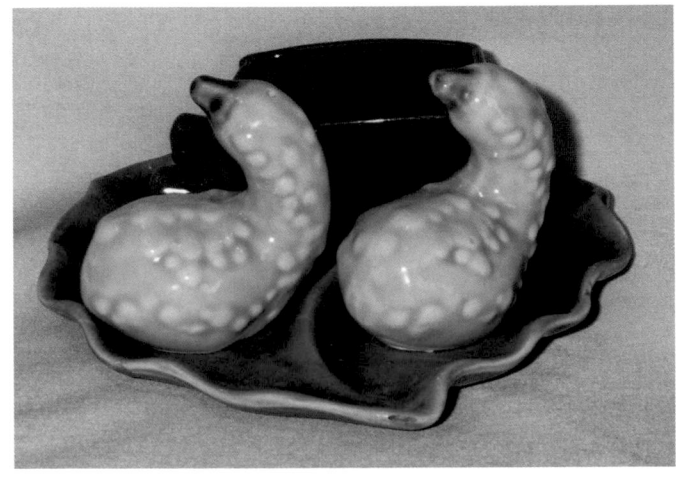

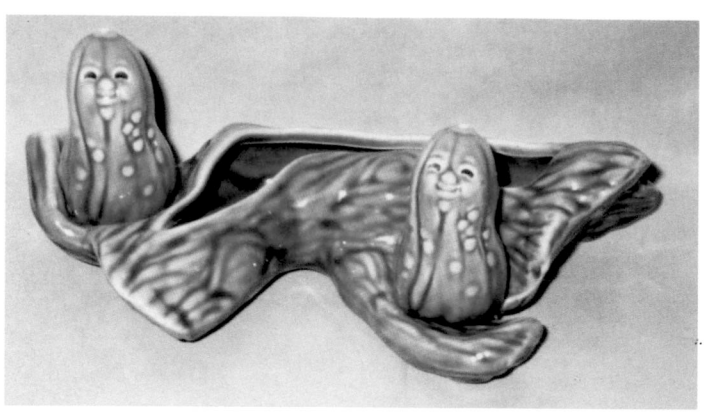

English walnuts. 1.5" high. $10-12.

Anthropomorphic cucumbers. 2" high. $12-15.

Peppers. 2.5" high. $12-15.

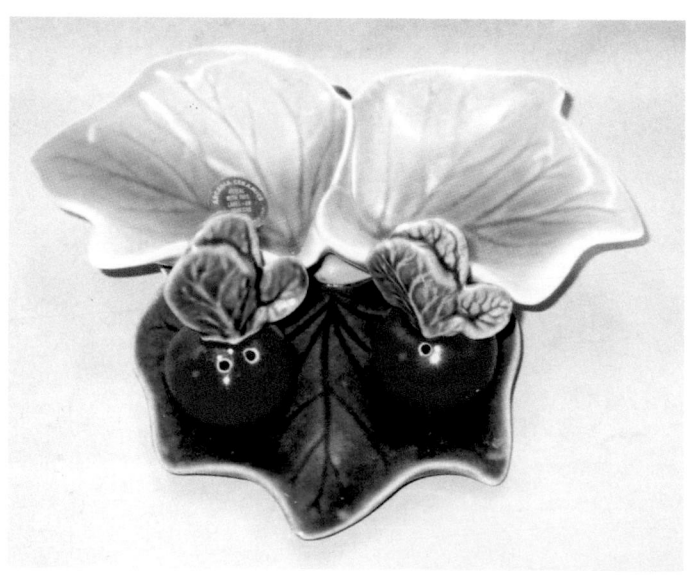

Tomatoes. 2.5" high. $12-15.

Radishes. 2" high. $10-12.

Potatoes. 1.5" high. $10-12.

Flowers
Flowers are priced, as usually found, without a tray.
Names of flowers are our best guess.

Chrysanthemums. 1.75" high. $10-12.

Daisies. 1.75" high. $10-12.

Lilies. 1.75" high. $10-12.

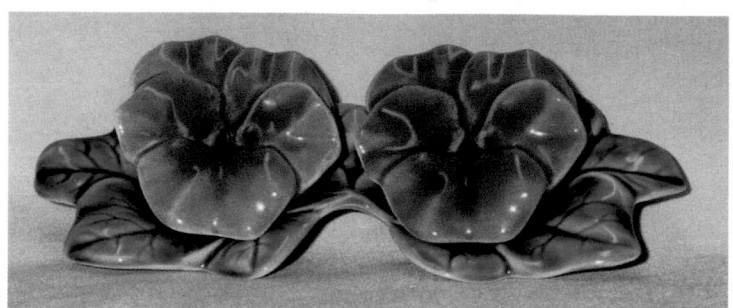

Pansies. 1.75" high. $10-12.

Roses. 1.75" high. $10-12.

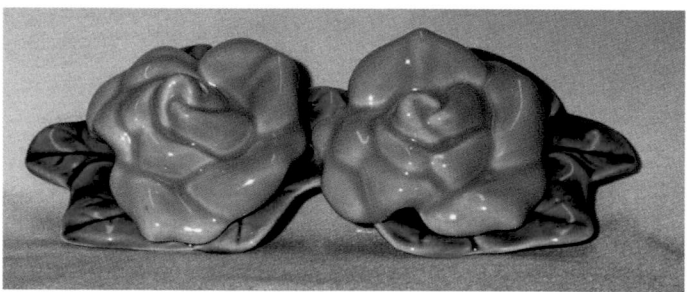

Tulips. 1.75" high. $10-12.

Wild rose. 1.75" high. $10-12.

Cosmos. 1.75" high. $12-15.

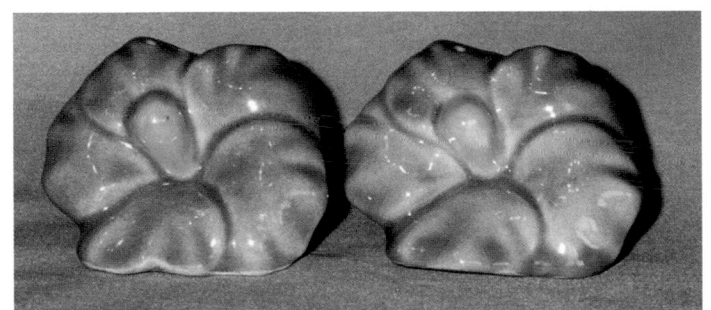

Antherium. 1.75" high. $10-12.

Morning glory. 1.75" high. $10-12.

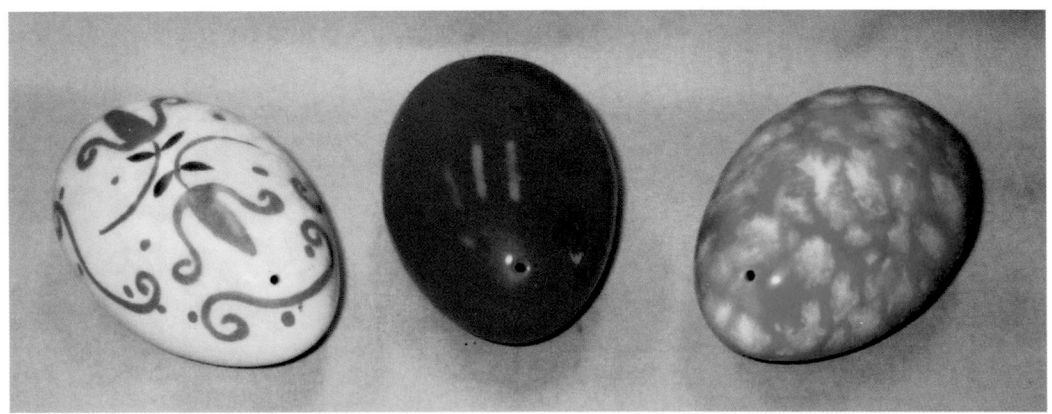

One-piece eggs. 3" high. Not priced. Very rare, gift from Mr. Bennett.

Chapter 2

California Originals

Founded in 1944 as Heirlooms of Tomorrow, by William D. Bailey, the company was located in Manhattan Beach and Torrance, California. The name was gradually changed in the 1950s and early 1960s to California Originals. At one time considered to be the largest art pottery in California, the company made a variety of products, including many cookie jars some with matching shakers. It was purchased by Harold Roman, in 1979, to combine with Roman Ceramics, and was closed in 1982.

Bear with beehive. 5" high. $20-25.

Rabbit with carrot. 5.5" high. $20-25.

Puppy with ball. 5" high. $20-25.

Owls. 5" high. $20-25.

Turtles. 5" high. $20-25.

Granny. 5" high. $20-25.

Sheriff. 5" high. $20-25.

Ark. 5.5"
high. $20-25.

Chapter 3

William H. Hirsch Manufacturing Company

The Hirsch company, located in the Los Angeles area, was listed in a 1946 directory as the maker of various art pottery figurines and earthenware. In November, 2003, Don Winton stated, "Hirsch was a jobber for Twin Winton but had his name [Hirsch] put on some items, which he sold." Don said that to his remembrance, both Twin Winton and Hirsch names would have been on those items.

Smiling bear. 5" high. $25-30.

Sailor elephant. 4.5" high. $30-35.

Lamb. 5.5" high. $20-25.

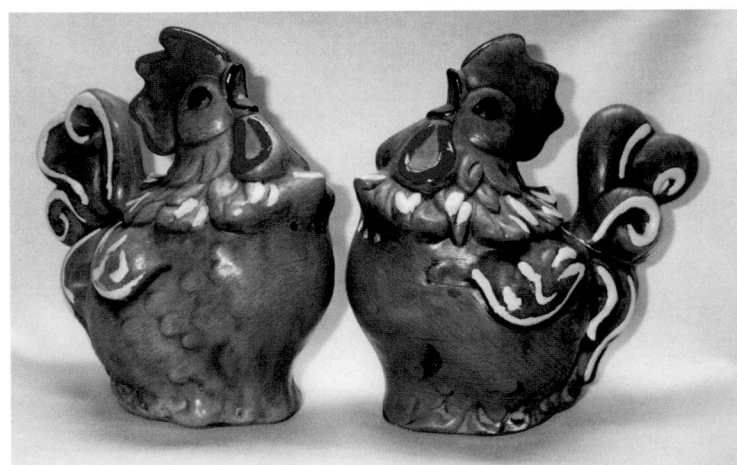

Rooster. 5" high. $25-30.

Chef. 6" high. $20-25.

Monk. 6" high. $15-20.

Wagon. 3.75" high. $15-20.

Chapter 4

Metlox Potteries

Metlox Potteries opened in 1927 as a division of another company. Their dinnerware production began in 1931, and their well-known Poppytrail tableware was introduced in 1934. Poppytrail was adopted in 1936 as the company's trade name to reflect California, the poppy being the state flower. When Evan K. Shaw, of American Pottery, purchased the Metlox company in 1946, it became prominent in the ceramics field. In 1958, Metlox acquired the trade name and some dinnerware molds when Vernon Kilns ended production, thereby starting the Vernonware Division of Metlox. Shaw passed away in 1980 and the company closed its doors in 1989. The "Pescado" line was the last dinnerware group produced.

Fish . 2" high. $20-25.

Pescado fish. 3.5" high. $55-60.

Duck. 4.5" high. $40-45.

California Provincial. 3.5" high. $12-15.

Red rooster and hen. 4" high. $25-30.

Chef Pierre mouse. 4" high. $60-65.

Mammy and Pappy. 7" high. Note: with blue or yellow trim, $125-150; with red trim, $140-165.

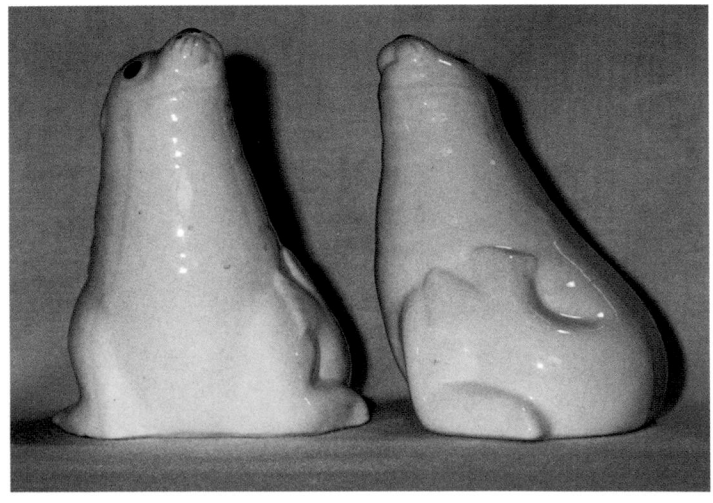

Sammy Seal. 5" high. $75-85.

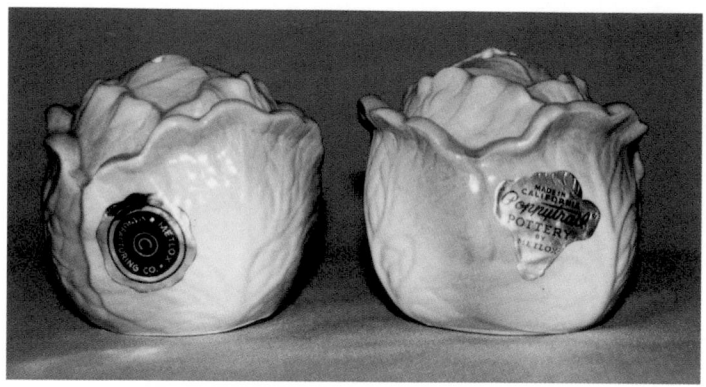

Cabbage. 2.5" high. $20-25.

Sculptured daisies 3" high. $15-18.

Strawberries. 1.5" high. $20-25.

Potato bins. 2.5" high. $18-20.

Tomatoes. 2" high. $20-25.

Watermelons. 2.25" high. $60-65.

Chapter 5

Treasure Craft and Pottery Craft
Shaker Sets
by George A Higby, author of Treasure Craft - Pottery Craft, USA

The highest-lived post-war California pottery (1947-1995) was Treasure Craft, a prolific producer of shaker sets. Started by giftware jobber Alfred Levin, in the garage of his Gardena, California, home, Treasure Craft initially contracted Laguna Beach pottery colony studios to make their ware, including novelty shakers. Clever, high-glaze designs included a flat tire with pump, inkwell with spill, and Indian in canoe. Though many were unmarked, some bore the firm's first mark, inkstamp "Treasure-Craft © SOUTH GATE, CALIF."

By 1949, the firm's Lucky California Sprites were so popular that Levin opened his own production facility in Compton, California. A Sprite shaker set, with unglazed bisque faces, joined the novelty lines. But 1951 tariff reductions favorable to Japanese potteries soon squeezed out many California firms, and Levin radically changed his lines.

(Authors' Note: Treasure Craft apparently stopped producing the go-with type sets around 1956, about the time of a fire at its first Compton factory.)

Defying the pastel 1950s, the firm opened a larger plant in Compton and switched to a rubbed-bisque finish called "Wood Stain." Matching sets of tableware replaced novelties, and sculpted lines, like Barrel and Fruit Wood, included stylized shaker sets. Marks were impressed in the mold, generally bearing the date; e.g. "19©57 TREA-SURE CRAFT-COMPTON" or "USA."

The change worked and the firm thrived, opening a Maui, Hawaii, branch in 1959. Devoted to souvenir ware, the Maui molds included a tiki god, pineapple, pirate/jug, puffer fish, and dolphin shakers, usually with stems that fit into a separate base. Though Levin provided all the design inspiration, art director Tony Guerrero and plant manager Ray Murray (formerly of Bauer) turned the concepts into 3-dimensional representations with consider-able detail.

By the late 1960s, wild bright colored glazes were reintroduced, this time as an interior compliment to the sienna outer edges. Shakers shaped as butterflies and mushrooms were given this psychedelic 1960s treatment.

As styles changed in the early 1970s, solid avocado Happy Face shakers gave way to new tableware lines on lighter backgrounds, with such transfer decals as Poppy and Butterfly, often marked "TC" or "TiC". A stoneware line called Pottery Craft [examples shown in this book on page 67], marked "IPC" or "IPiC", boasted a sculpted siesta man and howling wolf shaker sets.

By the 1980s, transferware dinner services dominated production, and shakers bore one of a few dozen designs, ranging from the country-style Blue Goose to high-style Midnight Sun. Production of Disney licensed products started with the Gourmet Mickey line and expanded to sculpted lines by designers who included Don Winton.

New designs generated huge orders for Treasure Craft, including shaker sets in the forms of Disney dwarfs, cacti, rag dolls, and cats. Having outgrown its four-block, 400-employee plant, Treasure Craft approached rival company Pfaltzgraff in 1988 to produce certain lines for them. Pfaltzgraff surprised them with a buy-out instead.

Metlox closed the next year [1989], leaving Treasure Craft as the last successful major California pottery. But problems integrating Treasure Craft with their Pennsylvania operations, and the post-NAFTA lure of cheap foreign labor caused Pfaltzgraff's sudden decision to shift all production offshore at the end of 1995. While several 1990s molds were sent abroad, all earlier molds were destroyed.

A 1952 catalog list, furnished by Mr. Higby, follows. The shakers pictured are our best interpretation of this list.

Authors' Note: The following information was on hang tags that accompanied Hawaiian-made items:

Today's Gifts, Tomorrow's Heirlooms

Treasure Craft of Hawaii, Designers & Manufacturers of fine Hawaiian giftwares

ALOHA. This item was especially designed to bring you pleasant and lasting thoughts of Hawaii - - of beautiful scenery - - exotic customs - - soft enchanting tropical nights. Aloha State - - a dream of never ending sunshine, palm trees waving over white sand beaches - - to relax and enjoy life where gentleness is a way of life. Aloha.

Authors' Note: Treasure Craft subsequently again operated as an independent company, with products made overseas. It then became part of Zak Designs, of Spokane, Washington. The Treasure Craft product line was discontinued in December, 2002.

For early sets, add $5 for gold trim.

Merchant's sign. Not priced.

Sprites. 3" high. $25-30.

TREASURE CRAFT

JAN. 1952

Prices subject to change without notice.

Treasure Craft Price List, 1952.

NO.	DESCRIPTION	PRICE PER DOZEN
H-89	Owl and Book s/p	7.20
H-90	Stove/Coffee Pot s.p.	7.20
H-91	Dog/Slipper s.p.	7.20
H-92	Birthday Cake/Present s.p.	6.00
H-93	Lipstick/Perfume s.p.	6.00
H-94	Surfboard/Rider s.p.	7.20
L-714	Dog/Bone s.p.	6.00
T-33	Mail Box/Letter s.p.	6.00
T-34	Stump/Ax s.p.	6.00
T-35	Rabbit/Carrot s.p	7.20
T-36	Cigarettes/Matches s.p.	6.00
T-37	Ink/stain s.p.	6.00
T-39	Bear/Beehive s.p.	6.00
T-40	Bowling Ball/Pin s.p.	6.00
T-41	Boxing Gloves/Bag s.p.	6.00
T-42	Outhouse/Catalogue s.p.	6.00
T-43	Toothbrush/Paste s.p.	6.00
T-44	Tepee/Drum s/p.	6.00
T-45	P'Tchin Woo s.p.	6.00
T-47	Paintbrush/Can s.p.	6.00
T-48	Crazy House s.p.	6.00
T-50	Baseball/Mitt s.p.	6.00
783	Horned Toad/Cactus s.p.	6.00
784	Sleeping Mexican/Cactus s.p.	6.00
787	Dog/Hydrant s.p.	6.00
788	Corn s.p.	6.00

NO.	DESCRIPTION	PRICE PER DOZEN
(T-60)	Stove s.p.	6.00
(T-61)	Egg/Skillet s.p.	6.00
T-61H	Ham/Skillet s.p.	6.00
(T-62)	Humpty Dumpty s.p.	6.00
(T-63)	Spray Gun/Fly s.p.	6.00
? T-64	Rolling Pin s.p.	6.00
(T-65)	Scoop s.p.	6.00
T-66		
(T-67)	Coffee/Donut s.p.	6.00
T-68	Toaster/Waffle Iron s.p.	6.00
T-69	Lamp/Book s.p.	7.20
T-70		
Pix T-71	Auto s.p.	7.20
T-72	Jockey Hats s.p.	7.20
(T-73)	Violin/Case s.p.	6.00
(T-74)	Briefcase/Hat s.p.	7.20
(T-75)	Santa Claus/Toys s.p.	7.20
Pix T-76	Binoculars/Case s.p.	7.20
(T-77)	Penquin/Igloo s.p.	6.00
T-78	Pie ala Mode s.p.	6.00
(T-79)	Guitar/Case s.p.	6.00
(T-80)	Eskimo/Igloo s.p.	6.00
(T-81)	Tortoise/Hare s.p.	7.20
(T-82)	Fireplace/Log s.p.	7.20
(T-83)	Television Set s.p.	7.20
(T-84)	Soap/Dish s.p.	6.00
Pix T-85	Suitcase/Valise s.p.	6.00
(T-86)	Pancake/Syrup s.p.	7.20
(T-87)	Banana Split s.p.	7.20

Treasure Craft Price List, 1952.

NO.	DESCRIPTION	PRICE PER DOZEN
(V-805)	Television s.p.	6.00
V-809	Squirrel/Acorn s.p.	7.20
(V-812)	Churn/Stool s.p.	6.00
(V-816)	Bread/Butter s.p.	7.20
Pix V-817	Thermos/Pail s.p.	7.20
V-818		
(V-819)	Turkey/Roaster s.p.	6.00
V-820	Football/Megaphone s.p.	6.00
(V-821)	Ice Cream Freezer/Cake s.p.	6.00
V-822	Boots/Creel s.p.	6.00
! V-823	Basket/Laundry s.p.	6.00
(V-824)	Block/Cleaver s.p.	6.00
V-825	Barn/Silo s.p.	6.00
(V-826)	Bean Pot/Pepper s.p.	6.00
(V-827)	Scrub Brush/Bucket s.p.	6.00
V-828	Tire/Pump s.p.	6.00
(V-829)	Money Sack/Safe s.p.	6.00
V-830	Nut/Bolt s.p.	6.00
V-831	Magnet/Bar s.p.	6.00
V-832	Plane/Square s.p.	6.00
(V-833)	Tent/Campfire s.p.	6.00
V-834	Pop/Popcorn s.p.	6.00
792	Pelican/Lighthouse s.p.	6.00
(794)	Red Whales s.p.	6.00
(795)	Salmon/Creel s.p.	6.00
796	Hammer/Anvil s.p.	6.00
(797)	Lighthouse/Tender s.p.	6.00
798	Indian/Canoe s.p.	6.00

Owl and book. 2.5" high. $15-18.

Stove and coffee pot. 4" high. $15-18.

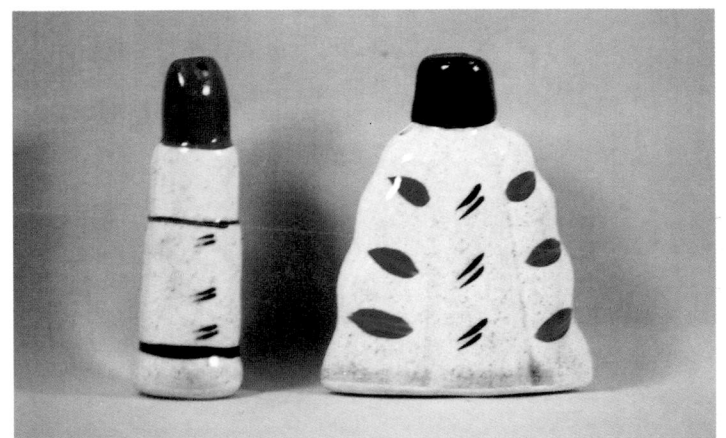

Lipstick and perfume. 2.75" high. $12-15.

Birthday cake and present. 1" high. $10-12.

Mailbox and letter. 4" high. $12-15.

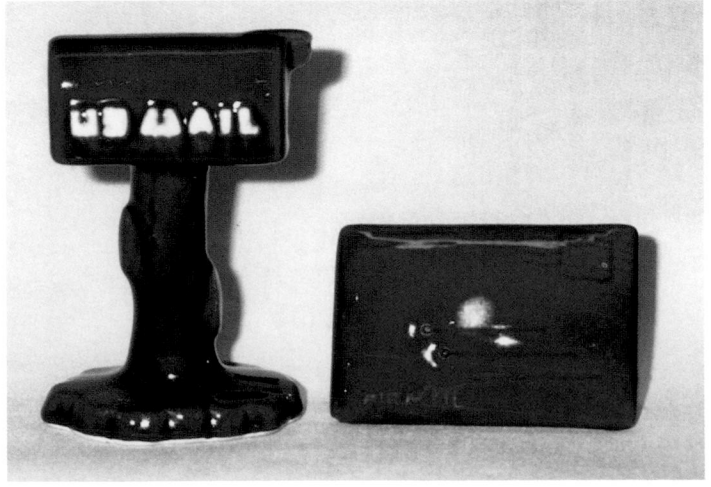

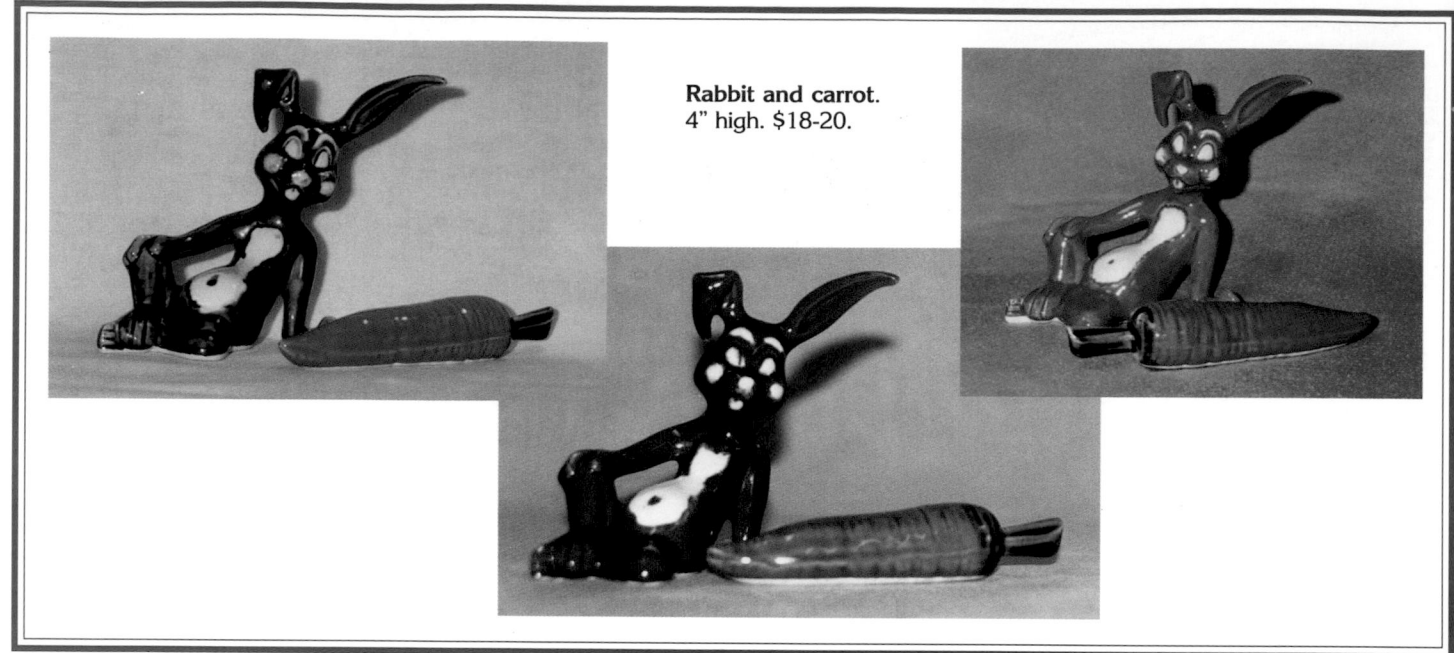

Rabbit and carrot.
4" high. $18-20.

Cigarettes and matches. 3" high. $12-15.

Ink and stain. 2" high. $18-20.

Axe and stump. 2" high. $15-18.

Bear and beehive. 3.25" high. $10-12.

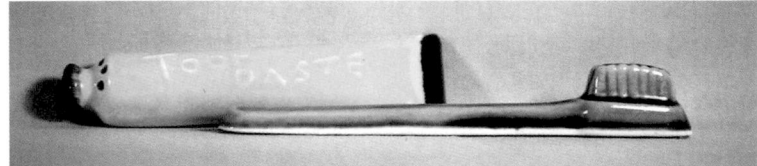

Toothbrush and paste. 1" high. $8-10.

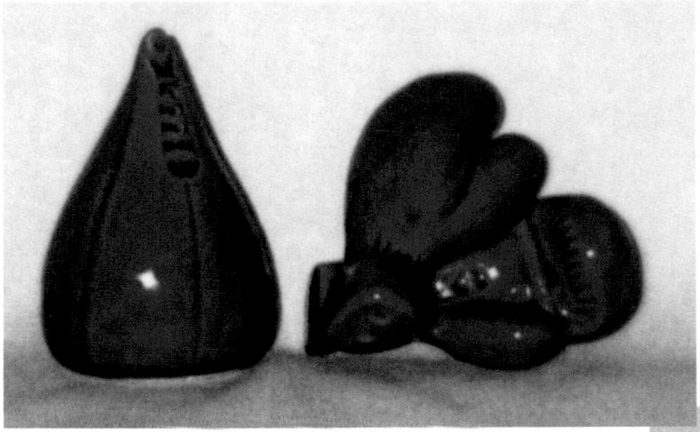

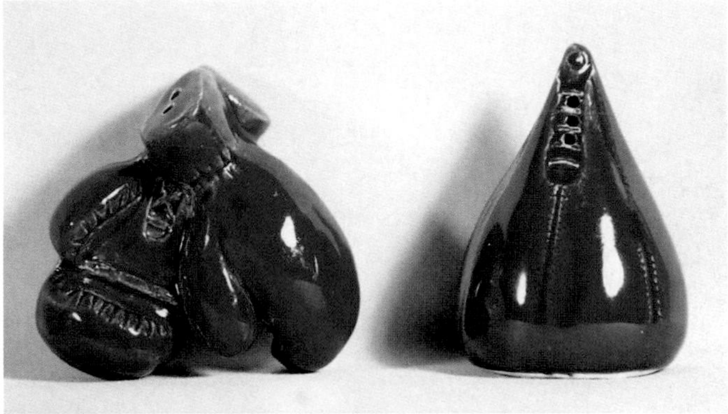

Bowling ball and pin. 4.5" high. $10-12.

Boxing gloves and bag. 3" high $12-15.

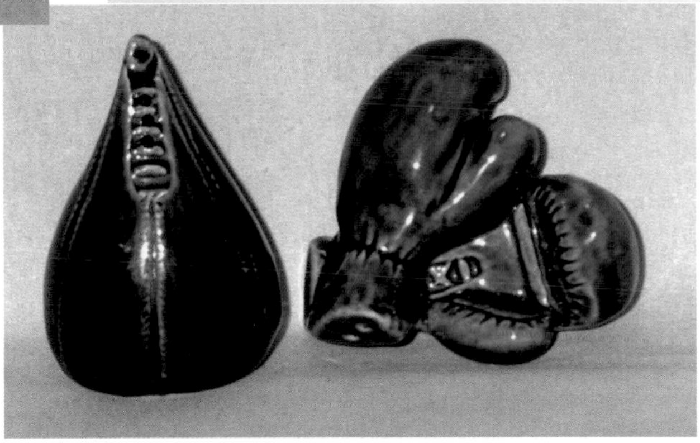

Outhouse and catalog. 3.75" high. $18-20.

Pitchin' Woo. 3" high. $25-30.

Tepee and drum. 4" high. $18-20.

Humpty Dumpty. 4.5" high. 12-15.

Ham in skillet and egg in skillet. 1" high. $12-15.

Paintbrush and can. 2" high. $10-12.

Baseball and mitt. 2.5" high. Left set, $12-15. Right set, $25-30.

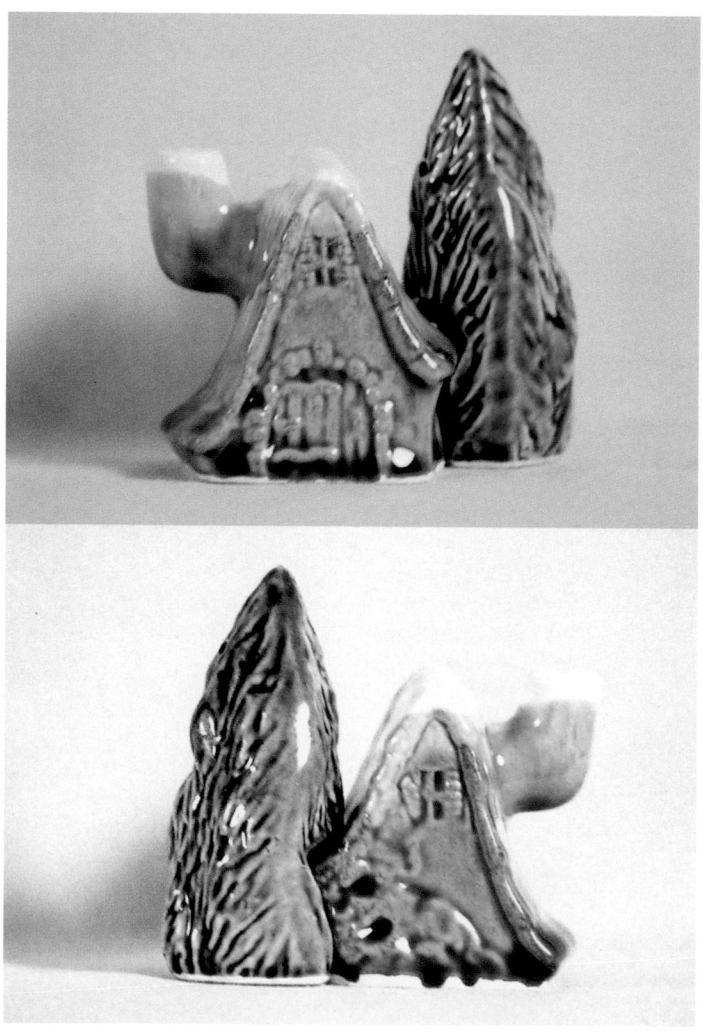

Crazy house. 3" high. $18-20. Front and back views.

Fish in skillet. 1" high. $12-15.

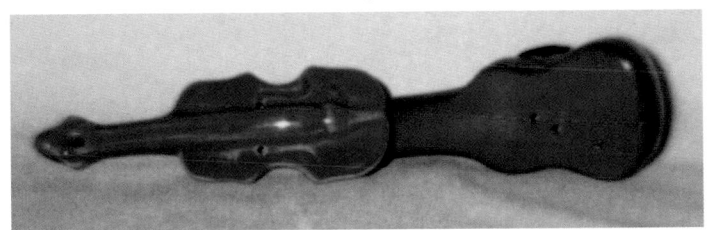

Violin and case. .75" high. $10-12.

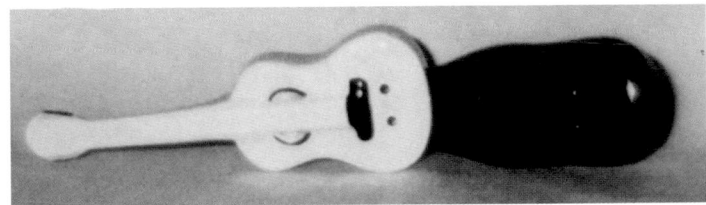

Guitar and case. 1" high. $12-15.

Pie a la mode. 1.75" high. $10-12.

Binoculars and case. 2.75" high. $12-15.

Eskimo and igloo.
2" high. $10-12.

Penguin and igloo. 2" high. $10-12.

Santa Claus and toys. 3" high. $20-25.

 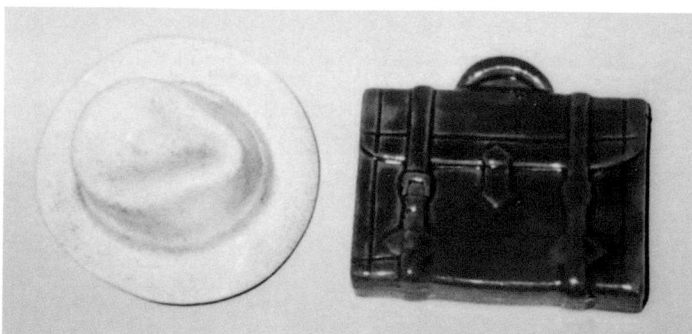

Briefcase and hat. 2" high. $12-15.

Soap and dish. 1.5" high. $15-18.

Pancakes and syrup. 2.25" high. $15-18.

Bread and butter. 1.5" high. $12-15.

Television. 4" high. $10-12. Note: TV screen added.

Television. 4" high. $10-12.

Sundae. 2.75" high. $12-15.

Banana split. 2" high. $12-15.

Squirrel and acorn. 2" high. $10-12.

Fireplace and logs. 2" high. $12-15.

Thermos and pail. 3.5" high. $12-15.

Churn and stool. 3.75" high. $12-15.

Block and cleaver. 1.75" high. $15-18.

Turkey and roaster. 2.5" high. $10-12.

Barn and silo. 3.75" high. $10-12.

Football and megaphone. 3.25" high. $12-15.

Scrub brush and bucket. 2.25" high. $10-12.

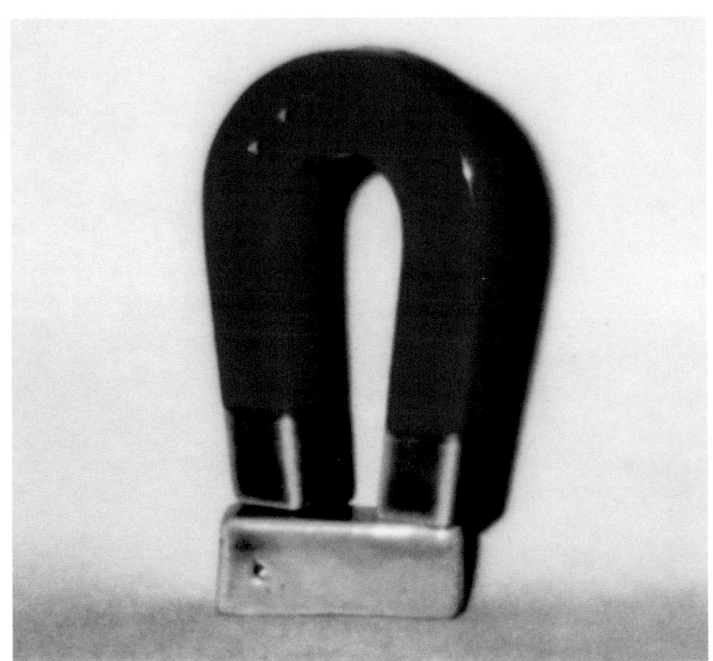

Magnet and bar. 3" high. $12-15.

Tire and pump. 3.25" high. $12-15.

Ice cream freezer and cake. 3" high. $12-15.

Basket with laundry. 2" high. $15-18.

Bean pot and pepper. 2" high. $18-20.

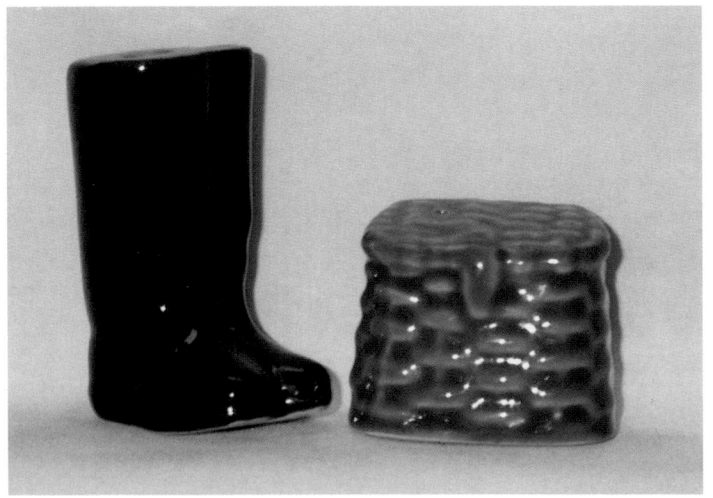

Boots and creel. 3.25" high. $10-12.

Money sack and safe. 2.25" high. $15-18.

Nut and bolt. 2.5" high. $12-15.

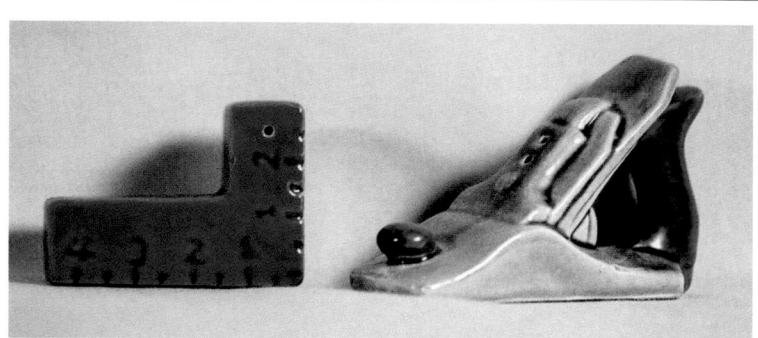

Plane and square. 1.75" high. $12-15.

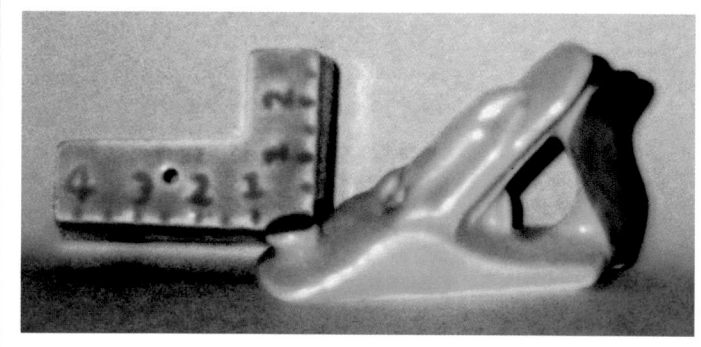

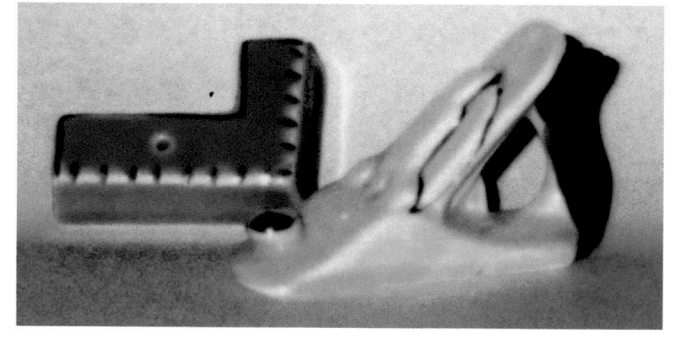

Pop and popcorn. 3" high. $12-15.

Lighthouse and tender. 3.25" high. $12-15.

42   Treasure Craft and Pottery Craft

Horned toad and cactus. 4" high. $15-18.

Sleeping Mexican and cactus. 4" high. $15-18.

Indian and canoe. 2.75" high. $12-15.

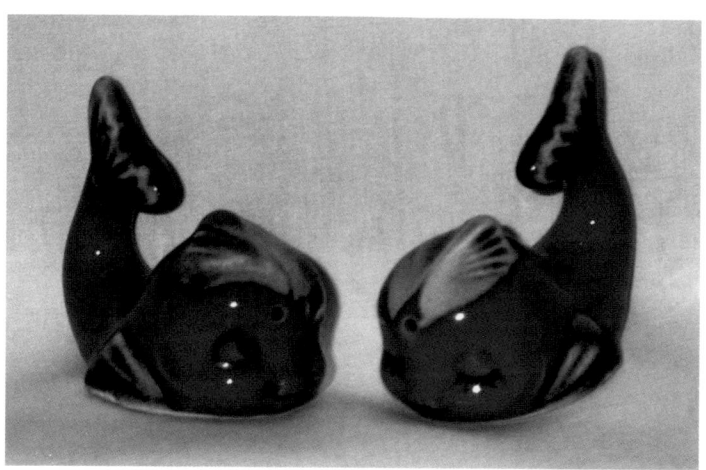

Red whales. 2" high. $10-12.

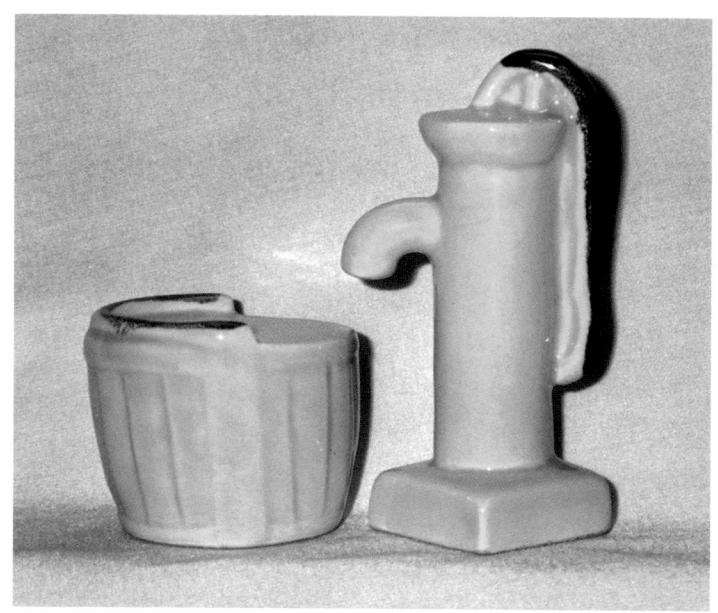

Pump and bucket. 4" high. $10-12.

Salmon and creel. 2.75" high. $10-12.

Gun and holster. 1" high. $15-18.

Hammer and anvil. 2" high. $12-15.

Flower in pot and green thumb. 2.75" high. $18-20.

Stove. 3" high. $10-12.

Coffee and donut. 2" high. $12-15.

Auto. 2" high. $12-15.

Lamp and book. 2.5" high. $12-15.

Scoop. 1" high. $10-12.

Spray gun and fly. 1.5" high. $18-20.

Rolling pin. 1" high. $10-12.

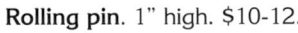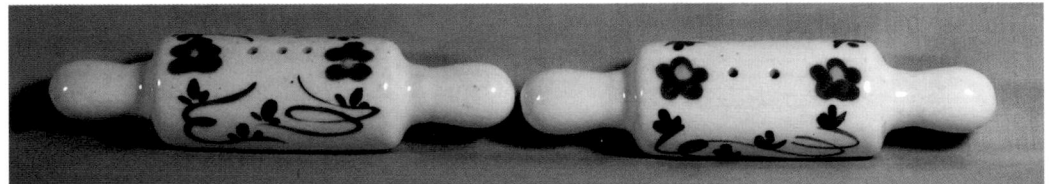

Bear and beehive. 4" high. $15-18.

Bears on tree. 4.5" high. $8-10.

Bears. 3" high, $12-15. and 4" high, $15-18.

Chickens. 5" high. $15-18.

Chickens. 4" high. $15-18.

Butterflies. 4.5" high. $12-15.

Butterflies. 4.25" high. $10-12.

Bluebirds. 4.25" high. $12-15.

Dolphins. 5" high. $12-15.

Whales. 4.5" high. $12-15.

Puffer fish . 3-3.5" high. $10-12.

Puffer fish before glazing. 3.5" high. Not priced.

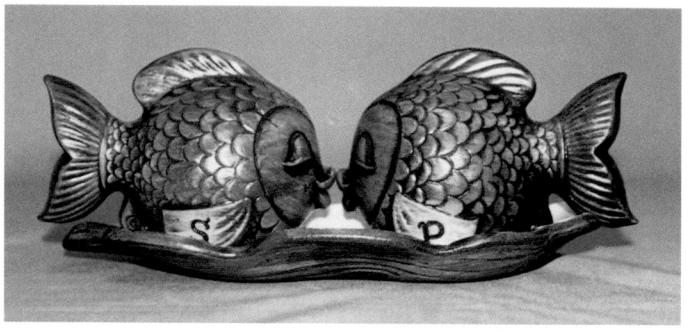

Frogs. 4.5" high. $15-18.

Angel fish. 3" high. $10-12.

Pigs. 3" high, $12-15. and 4" high, $15-18.

Rabbits. 3" high, $12-15. and 4" high, $15-18.

Rabbits. 5" high. $15-18.

Seahorses. 5" high. $12-15.

Roadrunner and cactus. 4" high. $10-12.

Owls. 4" high. $12-15.

Owls. 3" high. $10-12.

Owls. 4.5" high. $12-15.

Squirrels on tree. 4.5" high. $10-12.

Squirrel and acorn. 4" high. $12-15.

Vultures. 5" high. $20-25.

Hawaiian couple. 4.25" high. $12-15.

Natives. 4.75" high. $25-30.

Elves. 2.75" high. $15-18.

Beatniks. 3.5" high. $15-18.

Cowboy and cowgirl. 4.25" high. $12-15.

Jug and barrel. 2.5" high. $12-15.

Jug and barrel. 3.5" high. $18-20.

Treasure chest and cannon. 2.75" high. $18-20. Note: Different bases.

Sailing ships. 4.75" high. $12-15.

Skull and barrel. 3.5" high. $18-20.

Apple and pear. 4.5" high. $10-12.

Apple and pear. 3" high. $8-10.

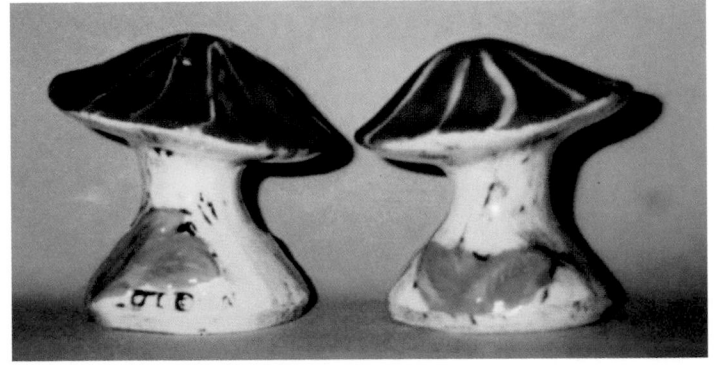

Mushrooms. 3" high. $12.-15.

Mushrooms. 3" high. $10-12

Mushrooms. 3" high. $10-12

Mushrooms. 3" high. $12-15.

Mushrooms. 3" high. $10-12

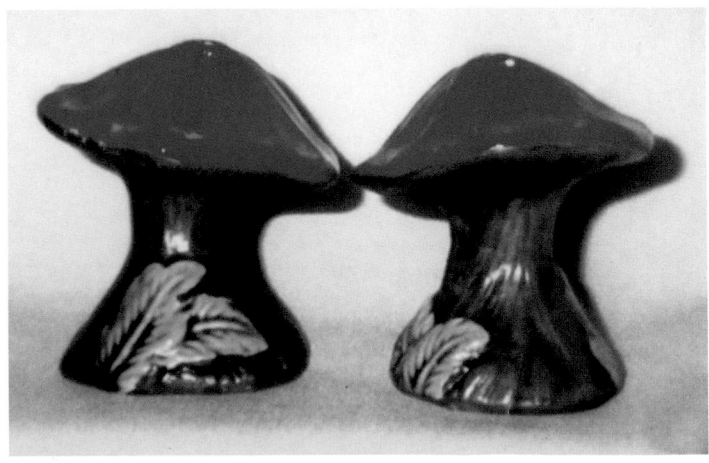

Mushrooms. 3" high. $10-12

Coconuts. 5" high. $10-12.

Pineapples. 4" high. $12-15.

Pineapples. Made in Hawaii. 4.25" high. $18-20.

Pineapples. 4" high. $12-15.

Tikis. 4.5" high. $15-18.

Flowers. 4" high. $15-18.

Boots. 2.5" high. $8-10.

Slot Machines. 3.5" high. $10-12.

Suitcases. Made in Hawaii. 2.25" high. $18-20. Front and back views.

Treasure chests. 2.5" high. $10-12.

Wagons. 3" high. $12-15.

Towers. 3" high. $5-8.

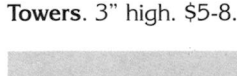

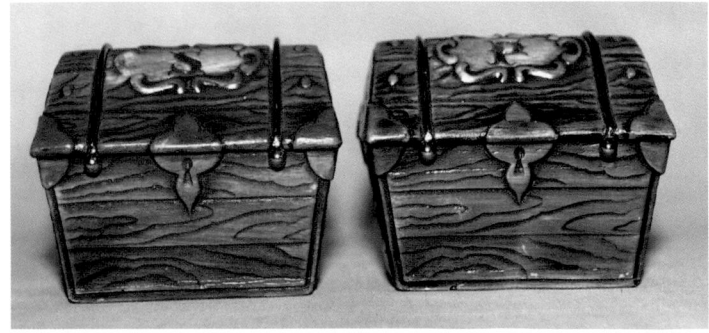

Treasure chests. 3" high. $15-18.

Bears. 3" high. $15-18.

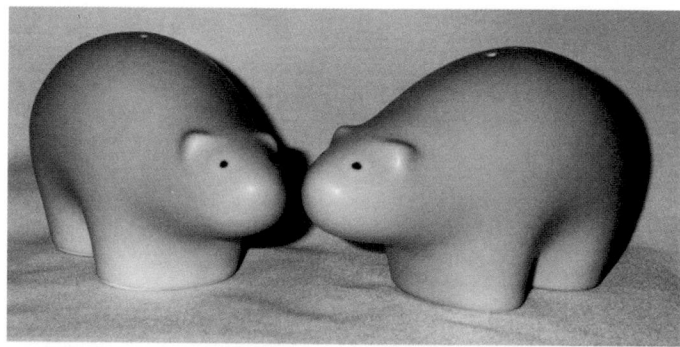

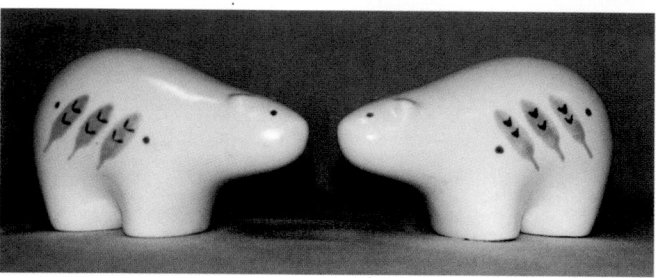

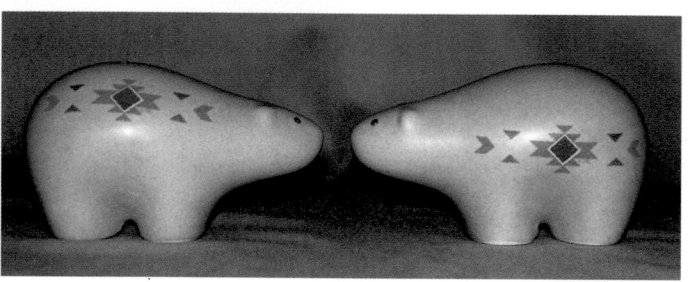

Bears. 4.75" high. $15-18.

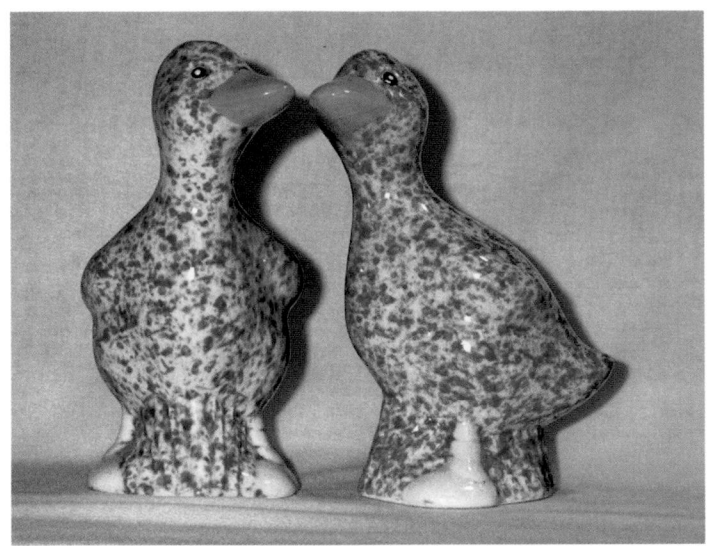

Ducks. 6" high. $15-18.

Chicks. 4.5" high. $15-18.

Cats. 4.25" high. $15-18.

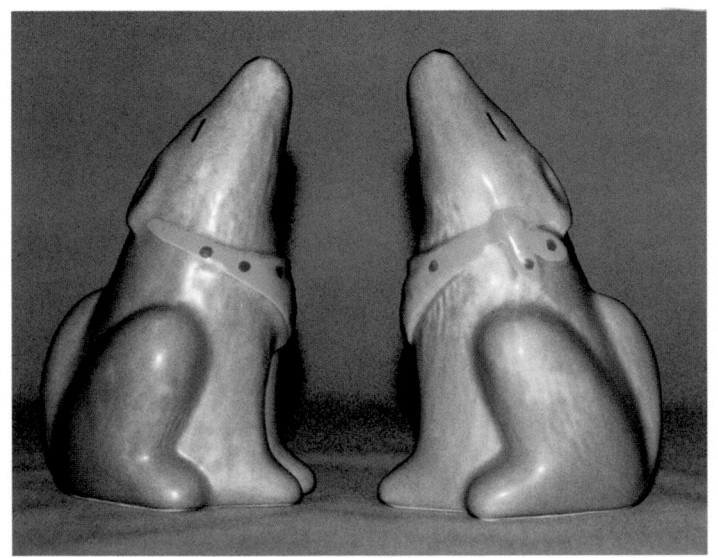

Coyotes. 4" high. $15-18.

Dinosaurs. 5" high. $20-25.

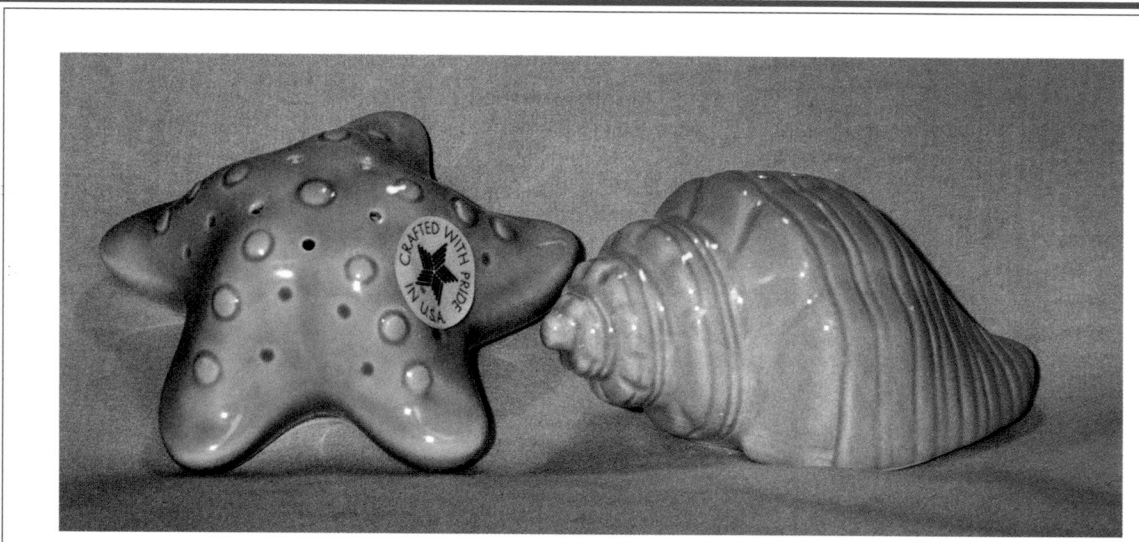

Seashells. 2.5" high. $15-18.

Rabbit and carrot. 4" high. $15-18.

Rabbit and watering can. 4" high. $18-20.

Smiley faces. 4" high. $12-15. Note: Correct sets are two of the same color.

Cowboy and Indian. 4.5" high. $18-20.

Orientals. 4" high. $20-25.

Chefs. 4.25" high. $15-18.

Boots. 4" high. $15-18.

Sugar and Spice. 5" high. $50-60.

Adobes. 2.5" high. $15-18.

Wagons. 3" high. $18-20.

Cactus. 4" high. $15-18.

Geese. 3.5" high. $10-12.

Milk bottles and tray. 4.75" high. $18-20.

Baskets. 3.5" high. $10-12.

Butterflies. 3.5" high. $10-12.

Christmas rose. 3.5" high. $10-12.

Floral. 3.75" high. $10-12.

Chickens. 3.75" high. $10-12.

Christmas geese. 3.5" high. $10-12.

Floral. $3.5" high. $10-12.

Disney-licensed sets

Pocahontas and Meeko. 3.5" high. $25-30.

Sneezy and Bashful. 4.5" high. $18-20.

John Smith and Pocahontas. 3" high. $15-18.

Simba and Nala. 3.5" high. $20-25.

Winnie the Pooh and Piglet. 3.5" high. $20-25.

Mickey Mouse. 5" high. $18 -20.

Genie and the lamp. 7" high. $25-30.

101 Dalmatians. 3.5" high. $15-18.

Mexicans. 4.75" high. $18-20.

Owls. 2.75" high. $15-18.

Geese. 3.5" high. $10-12.

Chapter 6

Twin Winton

Twin Winton Ceramics, founded in 1936 by twin brothers Don and Ross Winton, was located in Pasadena, California. The company was initially known as Burke-Winton, a partnership with Helen Burke who decorated and sold the products. Don designed the small animal figurines while Ross made the molds and managed the finances. In 1939, the partnership was dissolved and the brothers leased different quarters. From 1942 to 1946, operations were put on hold due to their war service. After 1946, an older brother, Bruce, joined the company and served as the business manager. He became sole owner of the company in 1952, when Don and Ross both left to become freelance artists. The pottery was moved to El Monte, where the well-known "wood finish" line, designed by Don, was produced. The business was moved again, to San Juan Capistrano, in 1964 and was closed in the mid-1970s. Ross passed away in 1980. Don has been a freelance designer for many clients, including Disneyland, Franklin Mint, Treasure Craft, Hanna-Barbera, Arcadia Ceramics, etc. Some of his current salt and pepper contributions are shown in this section.

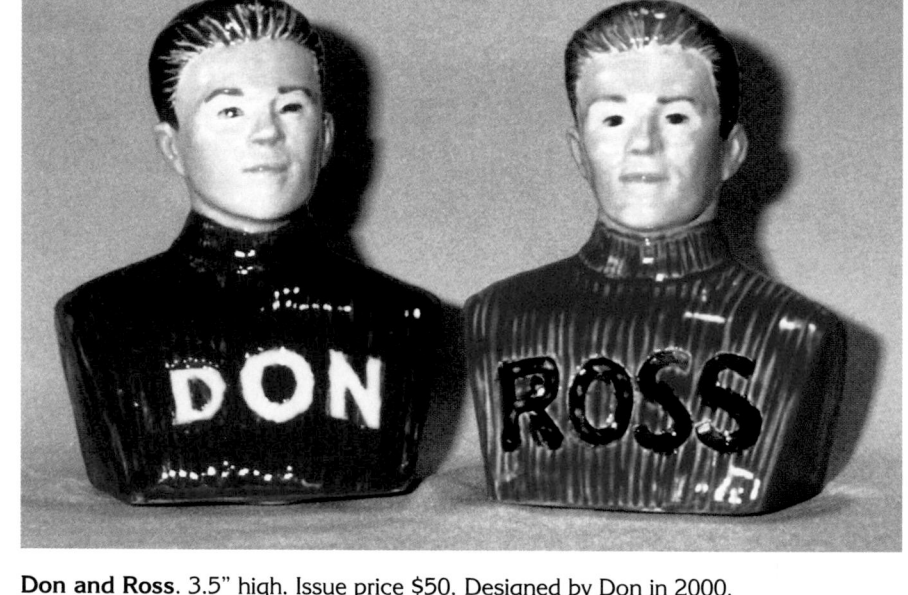

Don and Ross. 3.5" high. Issue price $50. Designed by Don in 2000.

Sign at the entrance to Diane and Ralph Bass's shaker room.

Marks.

Early Designs, 1930s-1940s

Bears. 3" high. $35-40 pair. Both pieces were signed by Don in 2000. The girl bear has H-42 painted on the bottom and the boy has H-44.

Bear, single. 3" high. $35-40 pair.

Left and below: **Bears**. 3" high. $35-40 pair.

Bears. 3" high. $35-40 pair. Nutmeg and cinnamon. Cinnamon has R-42 on the bottom. Nutmeg has R-44 and was signed by Don in 2000.

Raccoons. 2.5" high. $35-40 pair.

Rabbit single. 3" high. $35-40 pair.

Skunks. 2.5" high. $35-40 pair.

Chipmunks. 2.5" high. $35-40 pair.

1969 Twin Winton catalog cover, salt and pepper pages.

TWIN WINTON PLAQUE

THIS WHIMSICAL PLAQUE WILL BE INCLUDED WITH ALL INITIAL SHIPMENTS, FREE OF CHARGE. IT HAS PROVEN TO BE A VALUABLE SALES AID.

IMPORTANT

AFTER NINE YEARS OF MANUFACTURING OUR TWIN WINTON LINE IN A WOOD-TONE FINISH EXCLUSIVELY, WE NOW ANNOUNCE THE ADDITION OF 'COLOR'!

WE FEEL THIS WILL BE AN IMPORTANT ADDITION TO OUR ESTABLISHED LINE OF WOOD-FINISH PRODUCTS. THE ITEMS OFFERED TO YOU 'IN COLOR' HAVE BEEN CAREFULLY CHOSEN AND ARE PICTURED SEPARATELY IN THIS CATALOG.

WHEN ORDERING, PLEASE USE COLOR-CODE **LETTER** AFTER ITEM NUMBER:

A – AVOCADO

P – PINEAPPLE

O – ORANGE

R – RED

TW 184—Bear ....1.75 pr.

TW 166—Lamb ....1.75 pr.

TW 149—Cop ....1.75 pr.

TW 187—Rabbit ....1.75 pr.

TW 174—Squirrel ......1.75 pr.

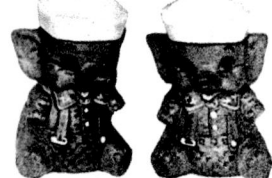

TW 186—Elephant ....1.75 pr.

TW 160—Butler ....1.75 pr.

TW 188—Donkey ......1.75 pr.

TW 144—Kitten ....1.75 pr.

TW 146—Pirate ....1.75 pr.

TW 176—Pig ....1.75 pr

TW 168—Rooster ......1.75 pr.

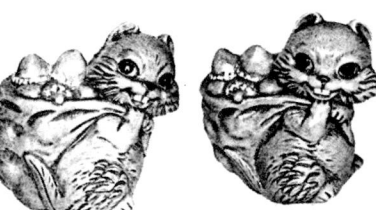

TW 145—Chipmunk ..1.75 pr.

TW 161—Hen ....1.75 pr.

TW 153—Teddy Bear..1.75 pr.

TW 177—Turtle ....1.75 pr.

Wood Finish Only

Wood Finish Only

SALT AND PEPPER SETS

SALT AND PEPPER SETS

TW 147—Dutch Girl....1.75 pr.

TW 172—Churn ....1.75 pr.

TW 170—Kitten ....1.75 pr.

TW 171—Dog ....1.75 pr.

TW 185—Friar ....2.00 pr.

TW 164—Poodle ....1.75 pr.

TW 169—Cow ....1.75 pr.

Wood Finish Only

TW 195—Bull ....1.75 pr.

TW 192—Raccoon ......1.75 pr.

THE FOLLOWING 9 SALT AND PEPPER SETS ARE NOW BEING MADE IN COLOR! AFTER **CODE NUMBER**, PLEASE USE COLOR LETTER.

TW 180—Dobbin ......1.75 pr.

TW 175—Goose ....1.75 pr.

Wood Finish Only

TW 165—Stove ....1.75 pr.
TW 165—A-P-R-O ......2.00 pr.

A—Avocado   P—Pineapple   R—Red   O—Orange

SALT AND PEPPER SETS

TW 181—Mouse ....1.75 pr.
TW 181—A-P-O ....2.00 pr.

TW 178—Hotei ....1.75 pr.
TW 178—A-P-O ....2.00 pr.

TW 191—Owl ....1.75 pr.
TW 191—A-P-O ....2.00 pr.

TW 190—Lion ....1.75 pr.
TW 190—A-P-O ....2.00 pr.

TW 159—Bucket ....1.75 pr.
TW 159—A-P-O ....2.00 pr.•

TW 157—Elf ....1.75 pr.
TW 157—A-P-O ....2.00 pr.

TW 138—Stove ....1.75 pr.
TW 138—A-P-R-O ......2.00 pr.

TW 158—Cookie Pot ..1.75 pr.
TW 158—A-P-R-O ......2.00 pr.

A—Avocado   P—Pineapple   R—Red   O—Orange

SALT AND PEPPER SETS

169—Cow .... 2.50 pr.

182—Shoe .... 2.50 pr.

197—Shack .... 2.50 pr.

198 Cable Car   2.50 pr.

141 Barn .... 2.50 pr.

165—Stove .... 2.50 pr.

Wood Finish Only

Wood-finish sets, 1950s-1970s

Colors added in 1969 were: avocado, gray, ivory, orange, pineapple and red. However, it appears that all sets were not available in colors. We believe some sets were never made in any color, just wood finish.

The names of the sets are those assigned by the company.

Note: Prices are for wood-finish sets. Sets of plain colors are usually priced higher.

The Collector Series (1974-1976) was introduced to offer colorful hand-painted items in limited editions, which command a premium price. Although this series was primarily cookie jars, some salt and pepper sets also were produced.

Ranger Bear. 5.5" high. $25-30. Note shield in left picture.

Sheriff. 5.5" high. $65-75.

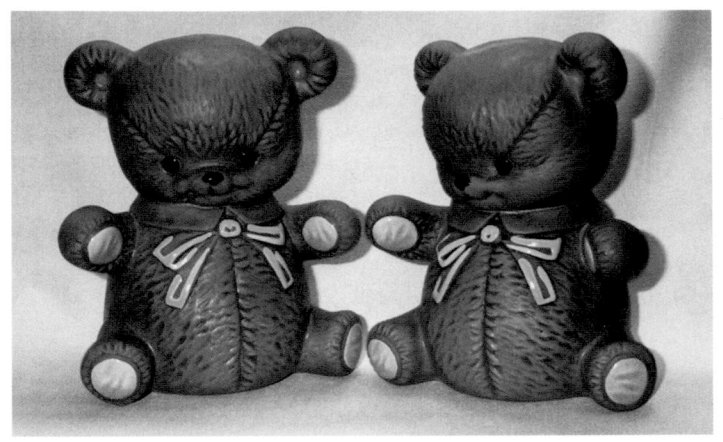

Teddy Bear. 5.5" high. $35-40.

Happy Bull. 5" high. $25-30.

Cow. 5" high. $35-40.

Chipmunk. 5" high. $40-45.

Persian Kitten. 5.5" high. $50-55. Note unusual bronze finish.

Persian Kitten. 5.5" high. $45-50.

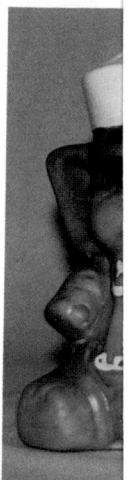

Kitten. 5.5" high. $45-50.

Churn. 6" high. $45-50.

Poodle. 6" high. $45-50.

Foo Dog. 6" high. $175-200.

Fr

Kangaroo. 6.

Dog. 5.5" high. $40-45.

Pirate Fox. 5.5" high. $45-50. Right set has paint added.

Mother Goose Collector Series. 6" high. $125-150.

Duck.

Duckling

Mother Goose. 6" high. $35-40.

Lamb. 5.5" high. $20-25.

Donkey. 5.5" high. $30-35.

Pig. 5.5" high. $45-50.

Owl. 5" high. $30-35.

Mouse. 5" high. $40-45.

Sailor Mouse. 5" high. $40-45.

Gunfighter Rabbit. 6" high. $45-50.

Lion. 5.5" high. $30-35.

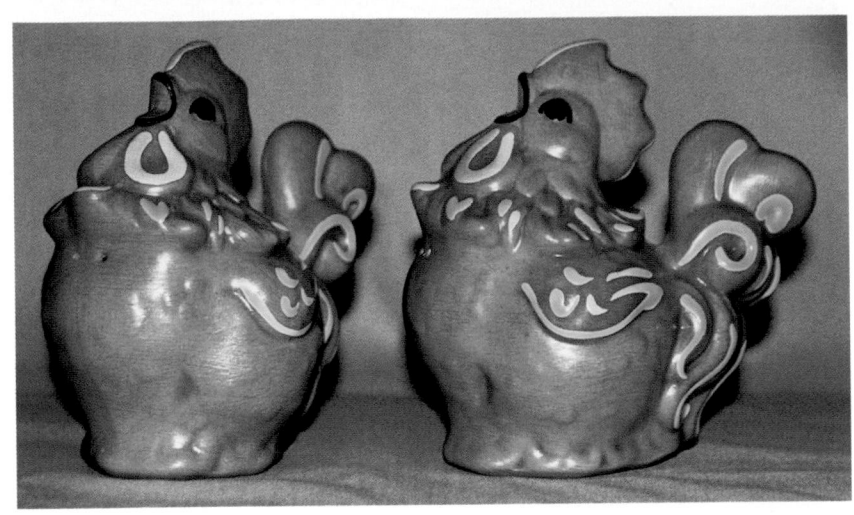

Rooster. 6" high. $25-30.

Raccoon. 5.5" high. $40-45.

Snail. 6" high. $100-125.

Squirrel. 5.5" high. $20-25.

Tommy Turtle Collector Series. 6" high. $125-150.

Tommy Turtle. 6" high. $55-65.

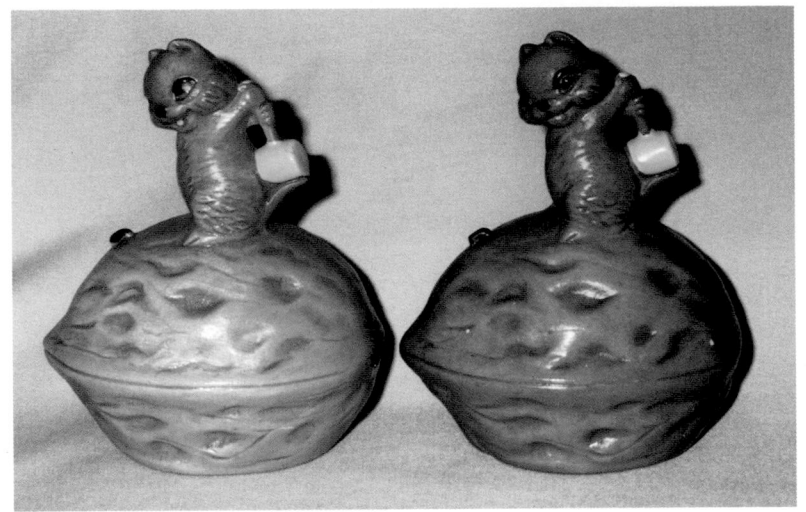

Nut. 6.5" high. $40-45.

Monk. 6" high. $15-20.

Butler. 6" high. $65-75.

Cop. 6" high. $25-30.

Dutch Girl. 5.5" high. $20-25.

Hawaiian Couple. 3.5" high. Unpriced. Extremely rare, very few made. Signed by Don in 2000.

Elf. 5.5" high. $25-30.

Elf. 5.5" high. $25-30. Left set has paint added.

Elf. 5.5" high. $25-30.

Hillbillies. 4" high. $15-20. Appear to have been mix and match.

Wampum single. 4" high. Unpriced. Very rare.

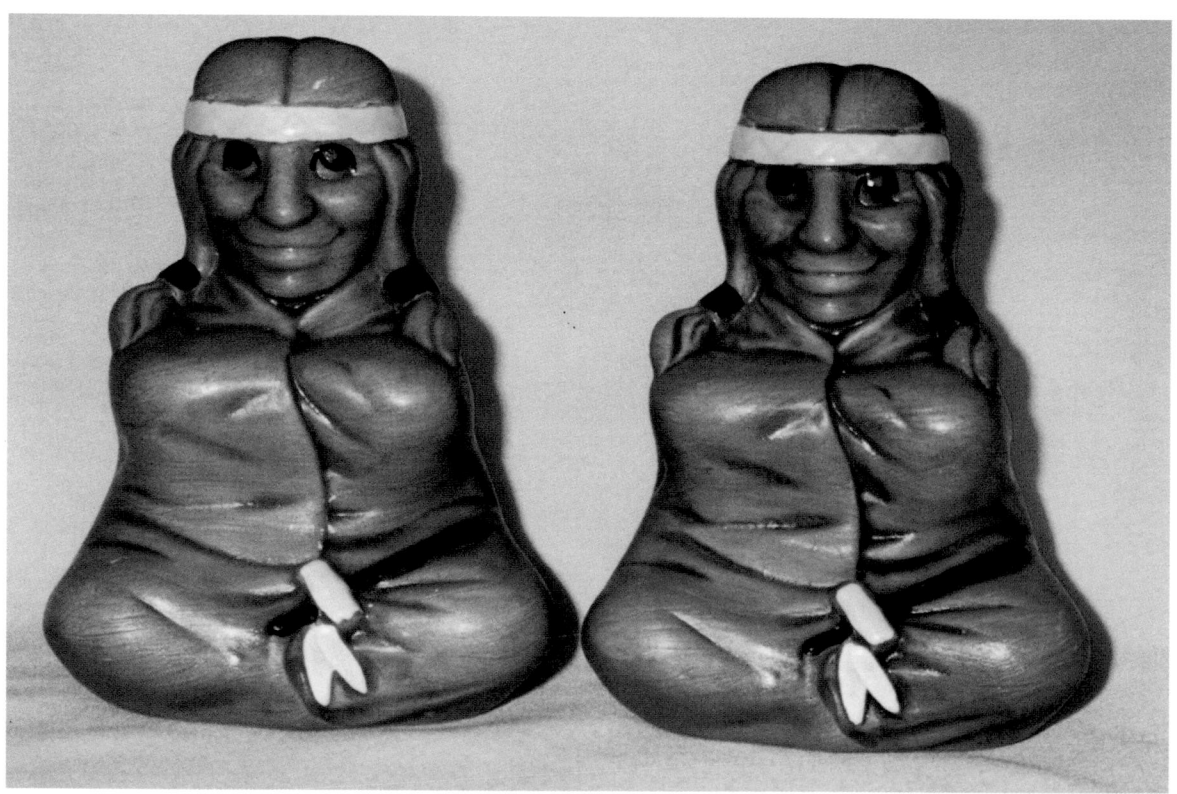

Indian. 5" high. $55-65.

Hotei. 6" high. $35-40.

Bucket. 4" high. $25-30.

Jack-in-the-Box. 6" high. $100-125.

Cable Car. 4.5" high. $55-65.

Cookie Barrel. 4.5" high. $75-85.

House. 5" high. $45-50.

Barn. 5" high. $25-30.

Barn. 5" high. $25-30. Left set has unusual color.

Barn. 5" high. $25-30.

Shack. 5" high. $45-50.

Cookie Pot. 3.5" high. $25-30.

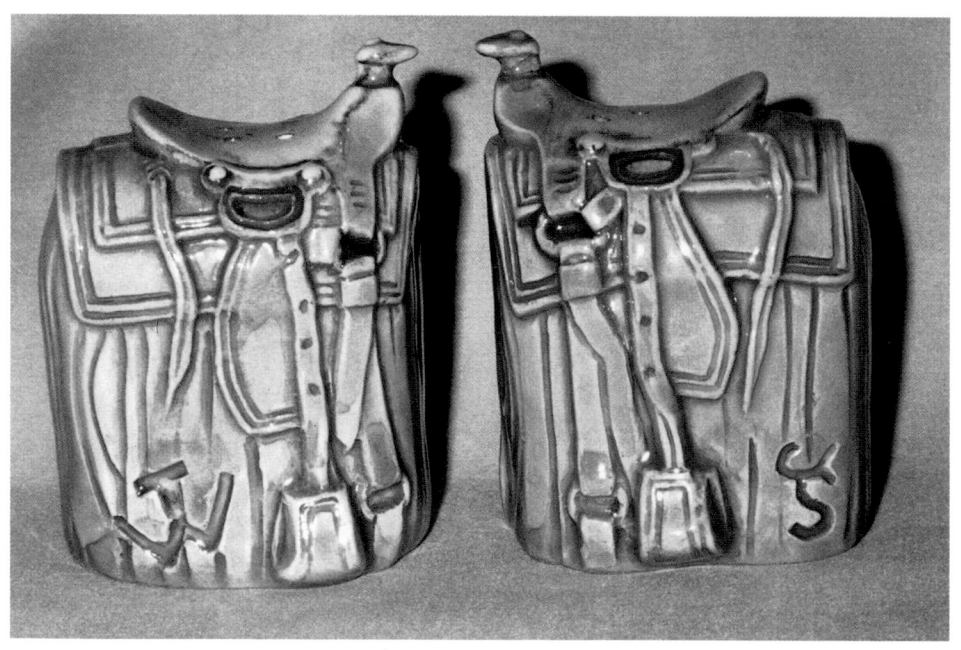

Saddle. 4" high. $25-30.

Shoe. 4.25" high. $40-45.

Pot-bellied Stove. 5" high. $30-35.

Stove. 4.25" high. $40-45.

Apple. 4.25" high. $90-100.

Pear. 5.5" high. $90-100.

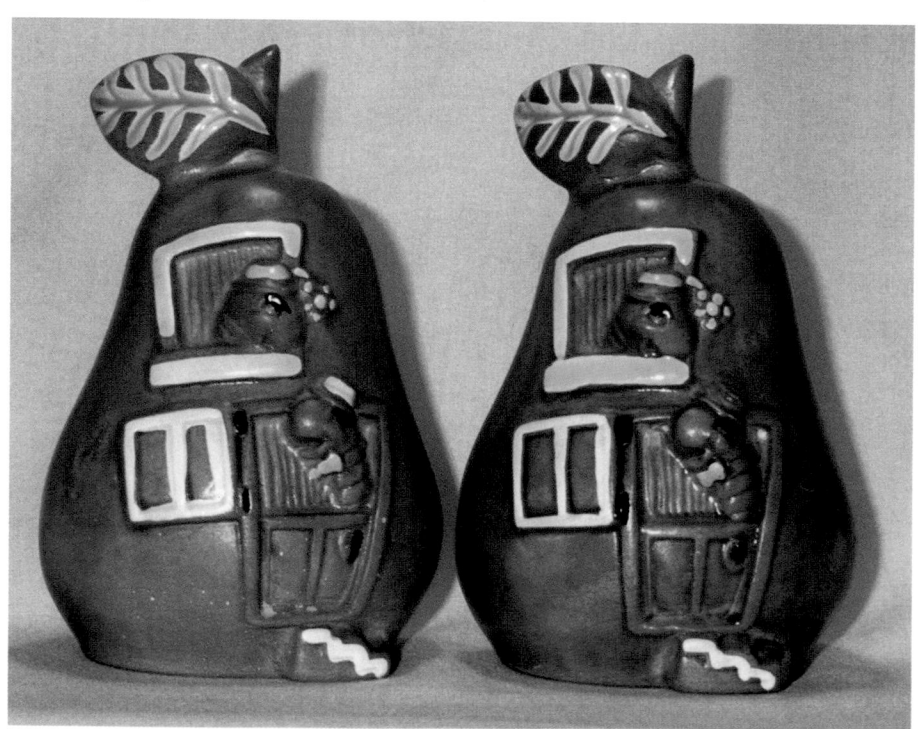

Famous Lover Series.

Lord Nelson and Lady Hamilton. 3.5" high. $90-100.

John Rolfe and Pocahontas. 3.5" high. $90-100.

Mary Todd, Abraham Lincoln, Ann Rutledge. 3.5" high. $75-85. Note: Lincoln is paired with either lady.

Robin Hood and Maid Marian. 3.5" high. $40-45.

Fido and doghouse. 4" high. Issue price $30.

Tammy and doghouse. 4" high. Issue price $30.

Polar bears. 4.5" high. Issue price $60.

Angels. 2.5" high. Issue price $30.

Sailor mouse. 2.5" high. Issue price $25.

Eskimo on igloo. 5" high. Issue price $85.

Panda. 2" high. Issue price $30.

Dinosaurs. 6" high. Issue price $75.

Dinosaur. 5" high. Note: single sample, not priced.

Dinosaurs. 3.5" high-4" high. Issue price $75.

Dinosaurs. 4" high. Issue price $75.

Part 2.
Other Potteries

Chapter 7
F & F Mold & Die Works

The F & F Mold & Die Works company, also known as F & F Plastics by collectors, was founded in 1946 by Otto Fiedler and his father, in Dayton, Ohio. Otto's father had previously founded the F & F Mold and Die Co. and had purchased some injection molding machines. Otto helped unpack the machines and was soon in the business.

The first advertising articles were made for the Quaker Oats Company as premiums for Aunt Jemima pancake flour. A complete line, including spice shakers, salt & pepper, cookie jar, creamer & sugar, and syrup pitcher, were made for the Aunt Jemima line. The Campbell Soup Kids, Millie and Willie (for Kool Cigarettes), Fido and Fifi (for Ken-L-Ration dog and cat food) are other sets made as premiums.

The Luzianne Mammy was made for the Luzianne Coffee Company. The red version of the Luzianne Mammy was thought to be a reproduction, however the set is marked on the bottom with "Langniappe of N.O." (New Orleans) and the "F & F Mold and Die Works" shield. It is felt that this set was made for the Langniappe Tea Company of New Orleans.

The mug and shaker combination, with faces, may have been made for a beverage company, but there are no markings to indicate this nor have we been able to determine a company.

Aunt Jemima and Uncle Mose. Left set 5" high. $40-50. Right set 3.5" high. $25-30.

Aunt Jemima

BY BETSY ZALEWSKI

Aunt Jemima pancakes were born in St. Louis, Missouri in 1889 by newspaperman Chris L. Rutt. Mr. Rutt named his self-rising pancake mix after a song named "Aunt Jemima". He had heard the song sung by two vaudevillians, Baker & Farrell. A few years later the R.T. Davis Milling Co. bought the business from Chris Rutt. The new owners launched Aunt Jemima pancake mix at the 1893 Colombian Exposition. The display booth was located in the Agricultural Hall and the company hired a black cook from Kentucky named Nancy Green to play the role of Aunt Jemima. She cooked over one million pancakes at the fair, demonstrating how to mix as well as cook them. She traveled the country as Aunt Jemima promoting the Davis Milling Co. pancake mix until her death in 1923.

The company had also invented a legend to go with the fictitious Aunt Jemima. They stated she was a smiling mammy cook who was a slave on Colonel Higbees plantation in Louisiana. She was famous in the south for her delicious, secret pancake recipe. According to the legend twenty years after the Civil War, the Davis Milling Co. purchased the famous recipe from Aunt Jemima and persuaded her to direct the preparation of the mix at the mill. This legend was used until the 1960's to promote Aunt Jemima pancakes.

In 1905 the Davis Milling Co. advertised their first promotion for Aunt Jemima flour. It featured a rag doll family ready to cut and stuff for 16¢ and four coupons and a climbing Aunt Jemima doll for 10¢ in stamps or coins and one package coupon. In 1949 an Aunt Jemima advertisement featured a rag doll family already stuffed for 75¢ and 3 box or sack tops. And in 1951 the 12" plastic F&F Aunt Jemima cookie jar was offered for $1.00 and one box-top. There were two different cookie jars made and both were boxtop coupon offers. Both were made by F&F Mold & Die Works Company of Dayton Ohio. The faces came in two different colors, brown and black. The black face jar was first offered in 1948 and the brown face jar in 1949. The cookie jars were a continuing promotion through 1951. Both are marked F&F and the black face jar has a value of $175-195 and the brown face jar has a value of $150-175.

In 1949 an Aunt Jemima six piece spice set was manufactured by F&F in red and white plastic. Each jar was 4" in height and the set included jars for Allspice, Cloves, Nutmeg, Ginger, Cinnamon, and Paprika. Also offered was a copper plated spice shelf with a scalloped edge, decorated with a steamboat scene. The shelf measured 12" x 4¼" and was only sold in 1949. A complete spice set with copper rack is valued at $125-140. In 1950 the copper plated shelf was replaced by a less expensive plastic one. It measured 12" x 2" and came in both red and white. At about the same time a three piece spice set consisting of Nutmeg, Cinnamon, and Paprika was offered for 50¢ and one box-top.

The figural Aunt Jemima and Uncle Moses salt & pepper shakers were box-top promotions offered in both the kitchen and range sizes. They were molded plastic made by F&F in 1948. The size of the table set is 3½" and has a value of $20-35. The range size measures 5¼" and has a value of $38-50.

The Aunt Jemima yellow plastic sugar with lid and Uncle Moses creamer was sold in 1949. Marked F&F, they were also a box-top offer costing 75¢ and 3 box-tops. In 1950 a green and blue sugar and creamer were manufactured.

The public did not like these because the colors did not match the other pieces. Consequently they are more difficult to find and command higher prices. According to one source the yellow sugar and creamer has an estimated value of $75-80, while the green set is valued at $100-125 and the blue goes for $110-150.

The plastic syrup pitcher started out as a box-top offer but as part of a marketing strategy to make Aunt Jemima the top selling pancake mix (Pillsbury was the leader at the time), the company began giving the syrup pitchers away by attaching them to the pancake boxes. The syrup is red & white plastic, marked F&F, circa 1949, 5¼" tall with a value of $25-45.

In 1948 a portable pancake grill (see picture) was used by the Quaker Oats Company as part of a traveling demonstration on "How to Make Aunt Jemima Pancakes". Set up at state and county fairs, pancakes were served on paper plates with Aunt Jemima's picture on them. As you can see in the picture,* a yellow plastic pancake shaker was attached to the side, it is marked Aunt Jemima and was also available in green or red. The grill had compartments for the kitchen & range salt and peppers shakers as well as the spice set.

* (not shown)

The Quaker Oats Co., a division of the American Cereal Co. bought the pancake recipe & the Aunt Jemima name in 1925. Today the smiling face seen on pancake and waffle boxes and syrup containers is that of Edith Wilson. In the 1950's, Quaker Oats hired Edith for commercials, personal appearances, and advertisements. She was born in 1897 and was a regular on the "Amos & Andy" show, both on radio and television. She was also a singer who recorded her first record in 1921 and a film actress who played with Humphrey Bogart in the movie "To Have & Have Not". Edith Wilson played the role of Aunt Jemima for over eighteen years.

Fifi and Fido. 3.25" high. $12-15.

Campbell Kids. 3.25" high. $20-25.

Anthropomorphic mugs. 3.25" high. $20-25.

Left set: **Langniappe of N.O.** 5" high. $90-100. Right set: **Luzianne Mammy**. 5" high. $75-85.

Millie and Willie. 3.5" high. $8-10.

The original McCoy Pottery was established in 1848 in Roseville, Ohio. Nelson McCoy, Jr. became the company's president in 1954. Best-known for its cookie jars, the company produced three salt and pepper sets that are known. Because the McCoy trademark was never registered by the original company, Roger Jensen of Tennessee was able to use the trademark, from 1991 on, to manufacture antique reproductions. Sets shown are "the real McCoy."

Cucumber and pepper. 5" high. $30-35.

Chinese cabbage single. 4.5" high. $30-35 pair.

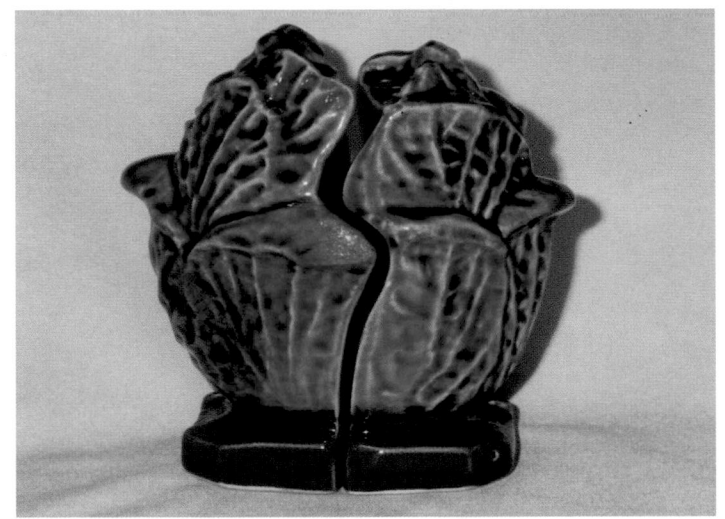

Cabbage, together and apart. 4.5" high. $30-35.

Chapter 9

Rossware
by Trish Claar

Several years ago, my husband and I bought a box lot of shakers at an auction. In the box were the bottom pieces of two ceramic hurricane lamp sets. Inscribed on the bottom of each piece was the word "ROSSWARE." As I started searching for information on these patents, I began to wonder if there was a connection between Howard L. Ross and "ROSSWARE." I am now pleased to report that there is.

Howard L. Ross was a businessman and inventor of many things, one of which was salt and pepper shakers. Some of his other accomplishments include "SODA-MIZER" bottle siphons, "LUSTRO-MAT" hot plate mats, and "CAP'N CORKY" bottle opener and cork screw.

In January, 1944, the Howard L. Ross Corporation was granted the right to use the trademark "ROSSWARE" on crockery, earthenware, porcelain, and ceramic tableware. The trademark statement also acknowledges that this mark "has been continuously used and applied to said goods in applicant's business since October 12, 1942." I understand this to mean that the trademark "ROSSWARE" could be found on items as early as the October, 1942 date and that the mark was used prior to registering it as an official trademark.

I have only seen four of the sets shown in the patent applications: The hurricane lamps, the angel, the dog and doghouse, and the water lily. Of these sets, some have been marked and some have not.

AUTHORS' NOTE: Based on the box for the kangaroo set, we believe the company was located somewhere in New York. Because of a label stating "Made by Stangl" on the kangaroo box, it is probable that Stangl made some or all of the sets for Rossware.

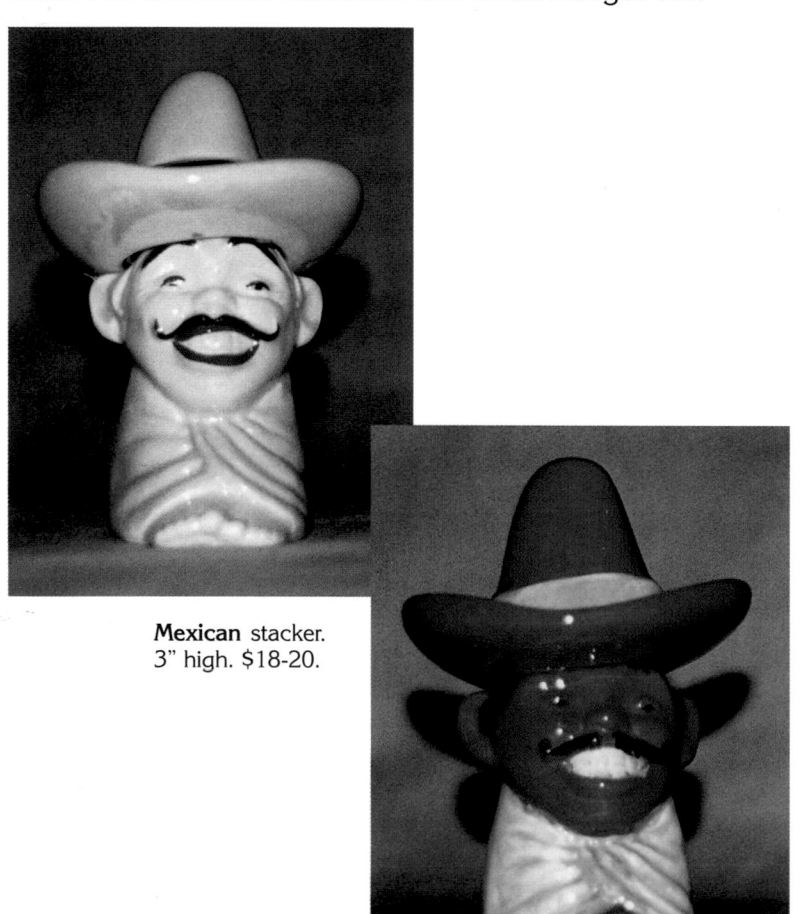

Mexican stacker.
3" high. $18-20.

Horse-head stacker. 4" high. $20-25.

Kangaroos. 4.5" high. $20-25.

Box for kangaroo set.

Angel stacker. 3" high. $18-20.

Girl stacker. 3" high. $18-20.

Lamp stacker. 3" high. $15-18.

Waterlily. 3" high. $18-20.

Six and nine stacker. 2.5" high. $18-20.

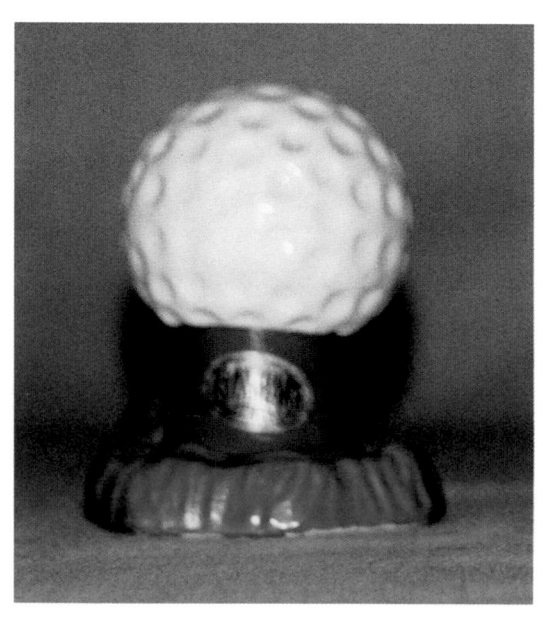

Golf ball on tee stacker. 3.25" high. $14-18.

UNITED STATES PATENT OFFICE

Nov. 10, 1942. H. L. ROSS Des. 134,282
COMBINED SALT AND PEPPER SHAKER
Filed Sept. 9, 1942

Nov. 10, 1942. H. L. ROSS Des. 134,280
COMBINED SALT AND PEPPER SHAKER
Filed Sept. 9, 1942

Nov. 10, 1942. H. L. ROSS Des. 134,281
COMBINED SALT AND PEPPER SHAKER
Filed Sept. 9, 1942

INVENTOR
HOWARD L. ROSS.
BY Paul A. Talbot.
ATTORNEY.

Rossware Patents

Rossware Patents

UNITED STATES PATENT OFFICE

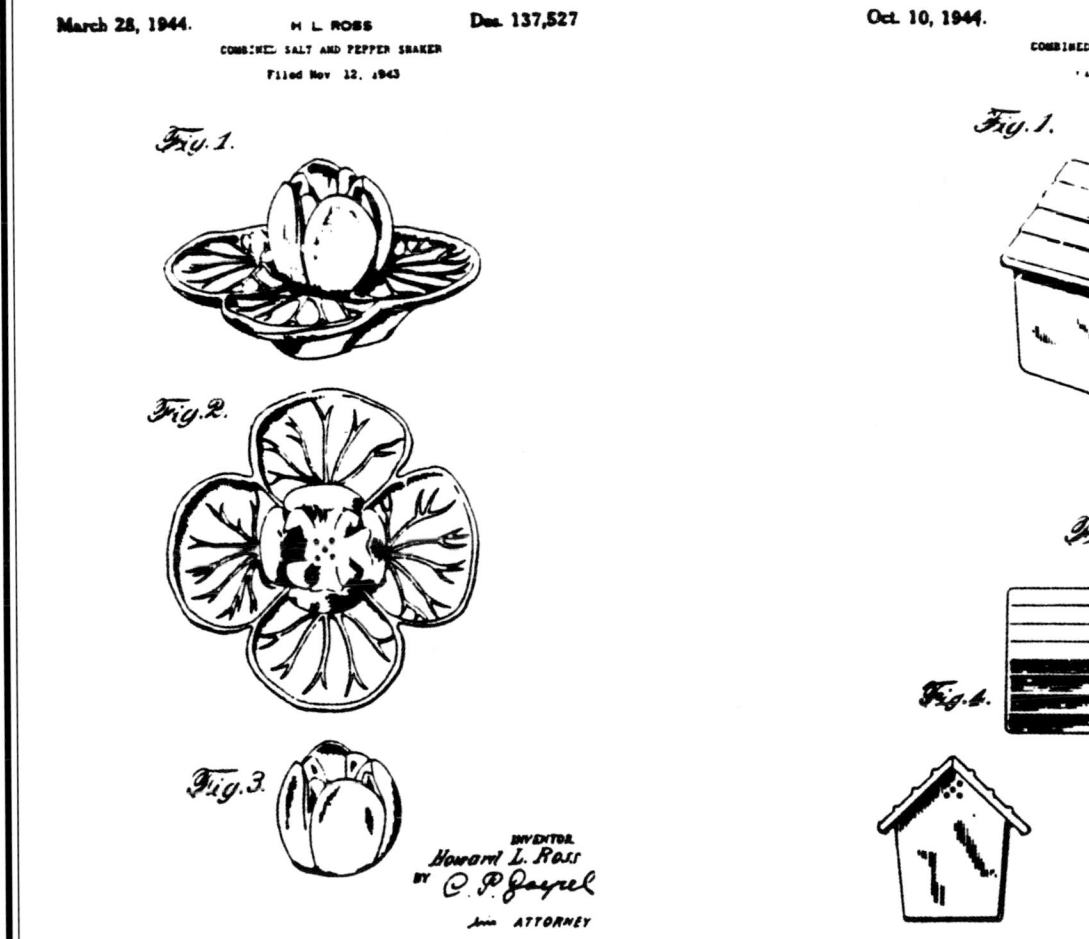

Rossware Patents

Chapter 10

Trevewood Pottery
by Bonnie Schwitzgable

The Trevewood Pottery was started in 1938, in Roseville, Ohio, by Ruth Prindle and her partner, Margaret Bolantz. The Roseville area was at the forefront of the Ohio Pottery movement due to the availability of clay fields and inexpensive sources of natural gas to fire the kilns.

Trevewood Pottery was initially a small business with no sales or marketing staff. They displayed the Trevewood line in a local restaurant window and soon orders exceeded expectations. The business continued to grow and additional employees were hired.

Trevewood's products consisted primarily of animal figurines and novelty salt and pepper shakers, many of which were trimmed in gold. The salt and peppers were made ready to be personalized with paper labels, for the souvenir and gift stores that purchased them. Most of the shakers had flat bottoms, designed to be sealed with scotch tape, and many of the sets were go-withs.

A variety of marks were used to identify the manufacturer and the following have been found on Trevewood shakers: "TREVEWOOD" (black inkstamp), "TP Co" (imprint), and "© TREVEWOOD". The imprinted marks are frequently in the glazed areas of the shaker and are hard to spot unless you are specifically looking for them. Many of the shakers were unmarked. You can often find identical sets where one set will be marked and one set will not. There is also variation in decoration, as some designs were decorated with and without gold trim. When comparing Trevewood sets side by side, you begin to notice consistencies in glaze colors with yellow, dark green, brown, black and light blue glazes being most prominent.

Ruth Prindle sold Trevewood Pottery to one of her employees in the mid-to-late 1950s, and it continued in operation for a number of years until the building which housed the pottery burned.

Note: Add $5 for gold trim.

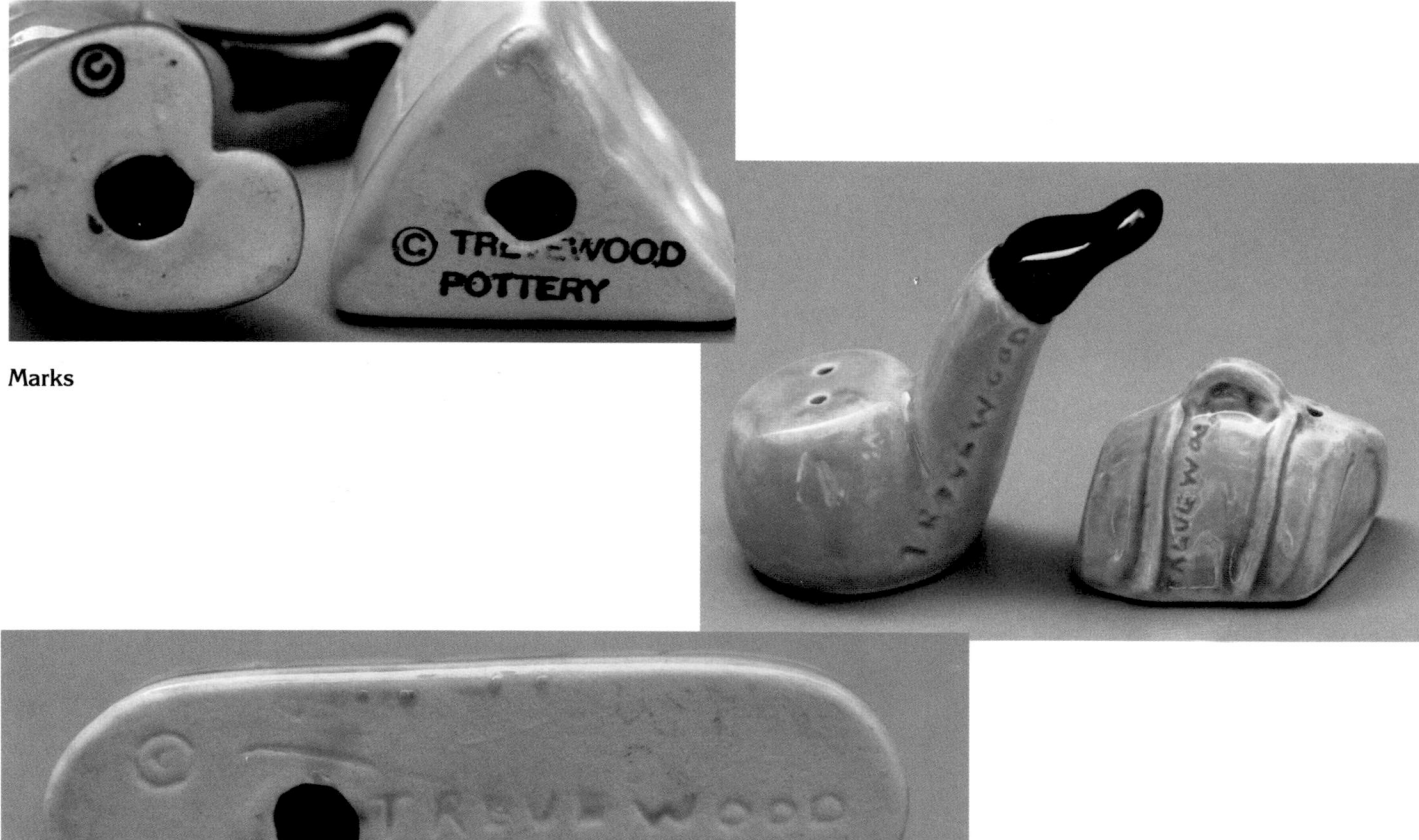

Marks

Chicken on nest. 2.75" high. $10-12.

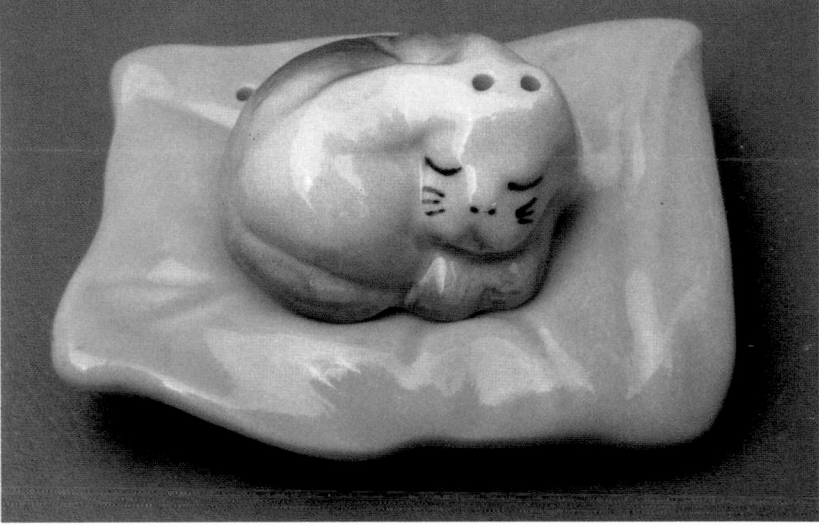

Dog on pillow. 1.75" high. $10-12.

Squirrels. 2.75" high. $12-15.

Mouse and cheese. 3.75" high. $8-10.

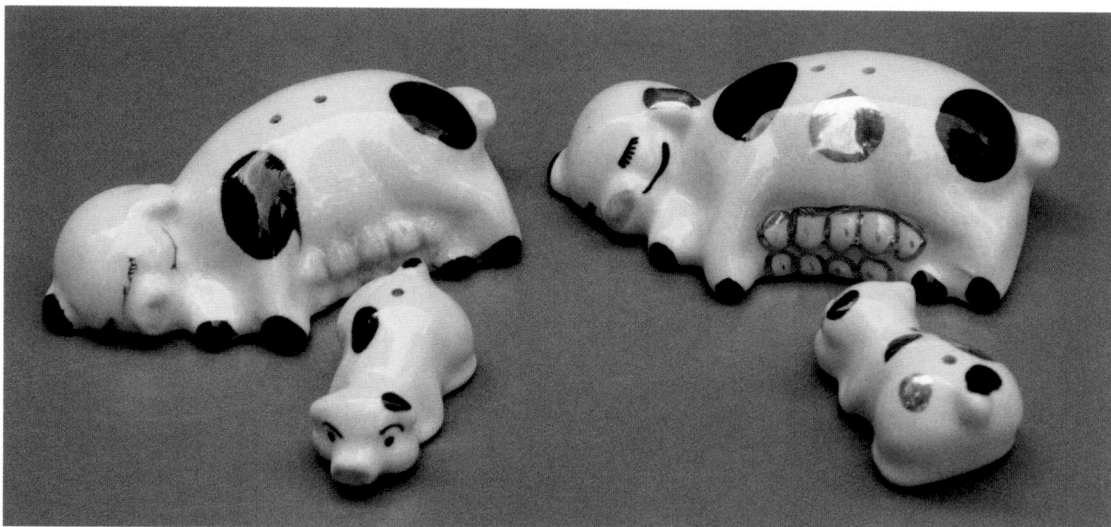

Pigs and piglets. 1.25" high. $15-18.

Hunter and rabbit. 3.5" high. $12-15.

Hitchhiker and bag. $3.5" high. $12-15.

Orientals. 2.5" high. $12-15.

Pipe on stand. 1.75" high. $10-12.

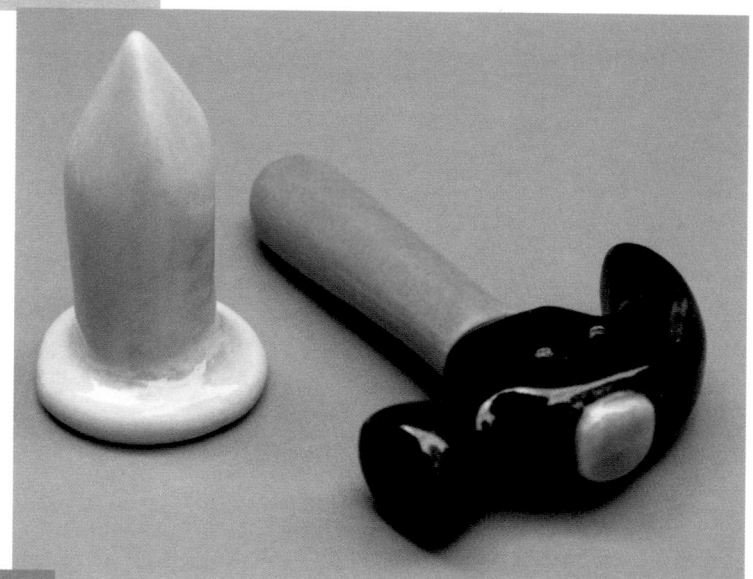

Hammer and nail. 2.75" high. $10-12.

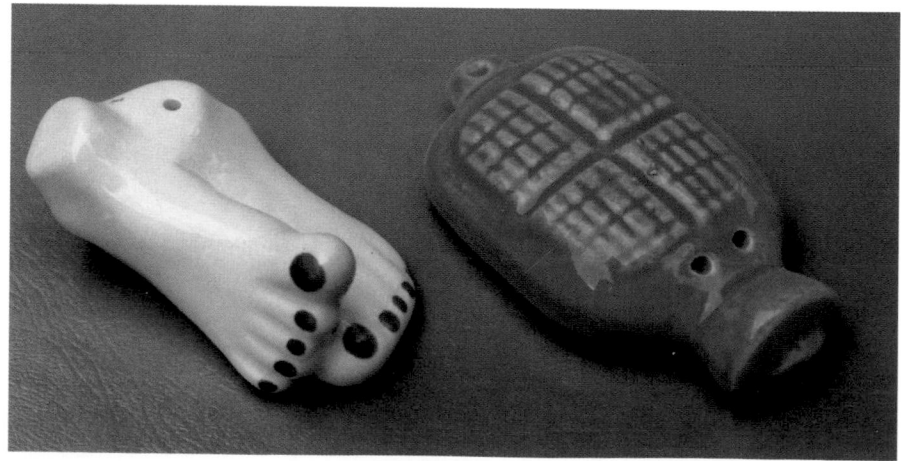

Shaving brush and mug. 2.75" high. $10-12.

Hot water bottle and feet. 1.75" high. $12-15.

The folowing sets are attributed to Trevewood by Steve Sanford, author of *Trevewood Pottery, A League of Their Own*.

Stump and hatchet. 1.25" high. $10-12.

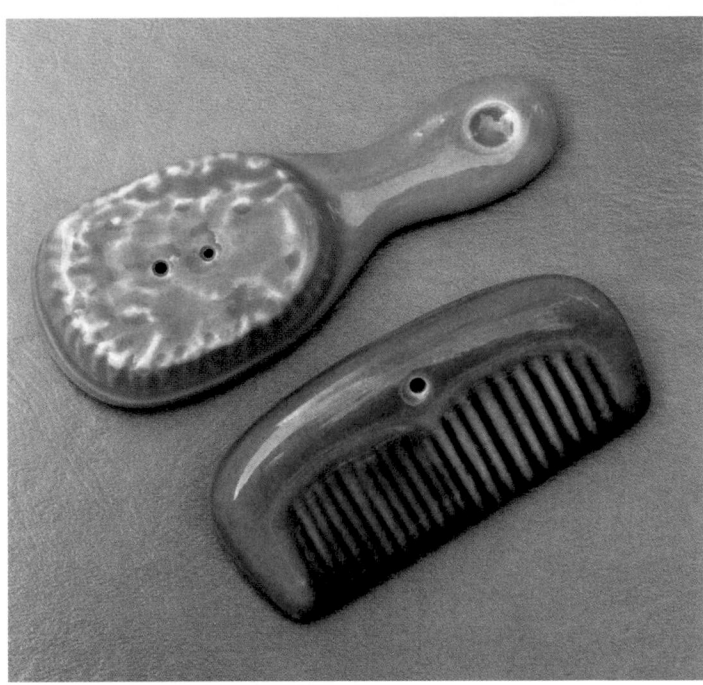

Brush and comb. 1" high. $10-12.

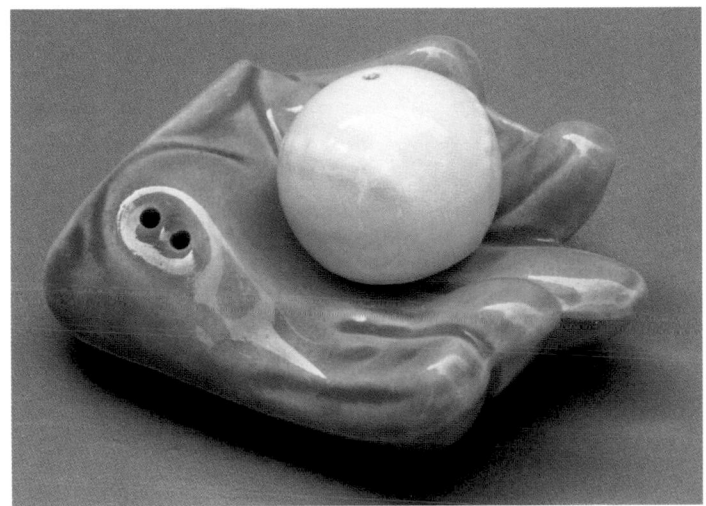

Baseball and glove. 1.75" high. $10-12.

Pig on platter. 2" high. $10-12.

Cigarettes and lighter. 2.5" high. $12-15.

Chapter 11

Rick Wisecarver

Rick Wisecarver, who was born in 1950, began his pottery career in his late teens. He designed and produced many cookie jars, some matching salt and pepper shakers and other items. His designs featured Afro-Americans, Native Americans, fairy tale and story book characters plus some animals. Pieces primarily were signed or initialled by Rick and incised "WIHOA'S": The "WI" represents Wisecarver, "HO" his mother's maiden name, Hoadley, "A" his relative, named Ault, and "S" his business partner, Richard Sims. Rick designed and produced the 1990 convention set for the Novelty Salt & Pepper Shakers Club. This set, as well as many others of his design, have several color variations. Unfortunately, Rick passed away in July, 2002.

Number One convention set sold for $450.

Afloat on the Mississippi, the 1990 club convention set. 600 sets made. 5" high. Issue price, $25. Current price, $175-$200.

Number one set with unique trim. $125-150.

Gone with the Wind. Produced as the alternate 1990 convention set. 4" high. Issue price, $40. Current price, $100-125.

Cotton Pickers condiment. 4" high. $90-100.

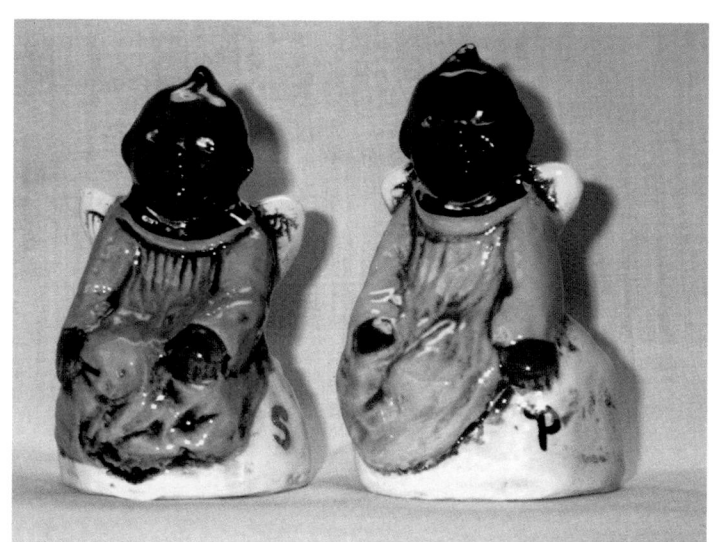 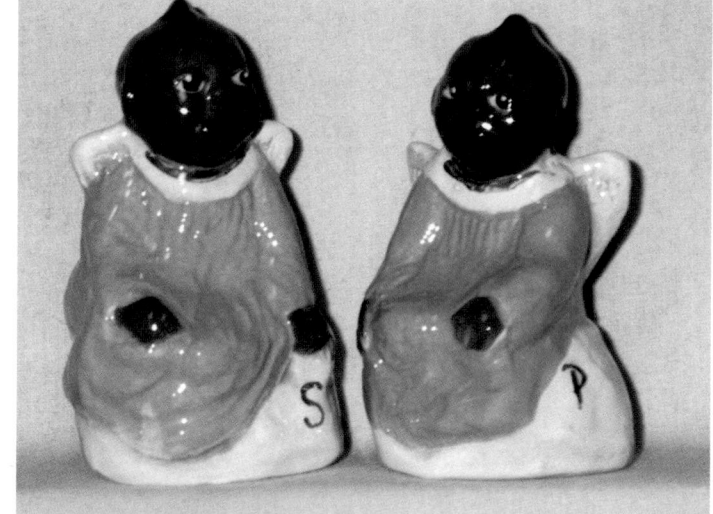

Angels. 3.75" high. $65-75.

 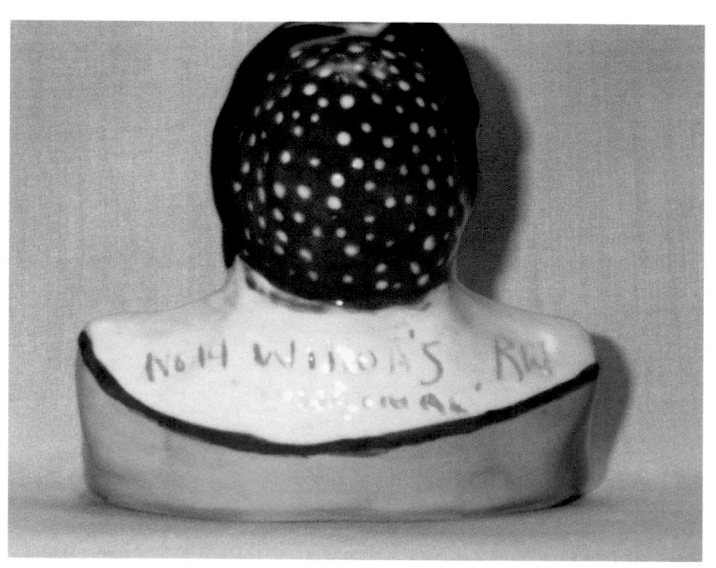

Mammy and Pappy. 3.5" high. $75-85.

Inscription on back of Mammy.

Watermelon Children. 5.25" high. $65-75.

Country Couple. 4.25" high. $65-75.

Mermaids. 6" high. $90-100.

Christmas Elves. 4.5" high. $65-75.

Little Red Riding Hood and wolf. 6" high. $65-75.

Little Red Riding Hood and basket. 5.25" high. $65-75.

Hansel and Gretel. 4.5" high. $65-75.

Hansel and Gretel. 4.5" high. $65-75.

Snow White and Witch. 5.5" high. $65-75.

Inscription on back of stump.

Owls. 5.5" high. $55-65.

Pig couple. 4" high. $45-50.

Cats. 3.5" high. $30-35.

Bibliography

Books

Chipman, Jack, *Collector's Encyclopedia of California Pottery, Second Edition*, Paducah, Kentucky, Collector Books, 1999.

Ellis, Michael L., *Collector's Guide to Don Winton Designs,* Paducah, Kentucky, Collector Books, 1998

Gibbs, Carl Jr., *Collector's Encyclopedia of Metlox* Potteries, Paducah, Kentucky, Collector Books, 1995.

Higby, George A., *Treasure Craft - Pottery Craft, USA,* Atglen, Pennsylvania, Schiffer Publishing Ltd. 2004.

Lehner, Lois, *Lehner's Encyclopedia of U.S. Marks on Pottery, Porcelain & Clay,* Paducah, Kentucky, Collector Books, 1988.

Roerig, Fred and Roerig, Joyce Herndon, *Collector's Encyclopedia of Cookie Jars, Book I, Book II and Book III,* Paducah , Kentucky, Collector Books, 1991, 1994 and 1998.

Sanford, Steve, *American Pottery Journal, Trevewood Pottery, A League of Their Own,* November, 1993.

Periodicals

Giftwares and Housewares Magazine, February, 1949.

Novelty Salt & Pepper Shakers Club Newsletter:

Vol. I, No. 3, "Patent Pursuit," Trish Claar, June, 1988.

Vol. IV - 1,"Arcadia Ceramics", Marcia Smith , February, 1991.

Vol. IV - 2, "Aunt Jemima," Betsy Zalewski, May, 1991.

Vol V - II, "More Arcadia Ceramics Identified," Carol Campbell, May, 1992

Ohio Chapter Newsletter, "Trevewood Pottery," Bonny Schwitzgable, February 1999

Treasure Craft List, 1952.

Twin Winton Catalog, 1969.